SpringerBriefs in Criminology

For further volumes:
http://www.springer.com/series/10159

C. E. Prowse

DISCARD

Defining Street Gangs in the 21st Century

Fluid, Mobile, and Transnational Networks

 Springer

C. E. Prowse
Department of Anthropology
University of Calgary
2500 University Drive N.W.
Calgary, AB T2N 1N4
Canada

ISSN 2192-8533   ISSN 2192-8541   (electronic)
ISBN 978-1-4614-4306-3   ISBN 978-1-4614-4307-0   (eBook)
DOI 10.1007/978-1-4614-4307-0
Springer New York Heidelberg Dordrecht London

Library of Congress Control Number: 2012941277

Printed on acid-free paper

Springer is part of Springer Science+Business Media (www.springer.com)

Preface

The introduction to the research findings that follow anticipates a number of questions fundamental to social analysis. Is it possible for a police officer / anthropologist / researcher who symbolized the "mainstream", to forge a trust with those who were indubitably gang "players"? How can an interviewer ever be sure how their questions are being understood by their informants: What did *you* think you thought you heard me ask? Is it possible to determine how gang leaders make their decisions concerning their following? How might have my profession as a police officer and my initial points of entry to my informants have influenced what became a protracted anthropological field study? And, how did I, as a researcher, ensure that my methods of making sense of the data did not interfere with the meanings provided by informants as part of their everyday interpretation of their activities?

My interest in gangs was awakened in the early 1990s in Calgary, Alberta, Canada where, while working as a police officer, Calgary sustained two unprecedented large-scale jewelry heists within an 8-month period. And, while this in itself would not necessarily be considered noteworthy in a large urban setting, what was particularly troubling about these armed robberies was that they were accomplished with precision timing, attracted little witness attention despite having occurred midday in the city centre, and then remained unsolved for a period of time as investigators searched for similar cases across the country that might lend insight into who might be responsible. While many in the policing community were convinced that these robberies were merely *ad hoc*—albeit very successful— others, including myself, were troubled by just how well orchestrated they were. And, while this author concedes that there can be *ad hoc* or spontaneous crimes, they are not usually this well executed at the group level; group-focused efforts generally require preplanning, patterned communication, and the ability to coordinate the liquidation of the proceeds of the crime so that all know they will share in the profits. The complete scenario is outlined in Chap. 1; my intention here is only to situate this experience within the context of the research that followed.

My formal research into the structure and organization of "new-age" street gangs began when I pursued graduate study in the early 1990s and my laboratory became the Southern Ontario corridor; a research site that was selected as a result of continuing police investigation into the armed robberies previously described, and that would ultimately be solved in that jurisdiction as a result of a gang-related triple homicide. Little did I realize at the time, that this research would continue for many years thereafter in other Canadian-based venues; frequently on an intermittent basis pursuant to new avenues of research in need of pursuit, or oftentimes determined by the availability of new informants; some now having been released from incarceration and introduced to me through "friends of friends". While many of the informants consulted during this extended period of research were indubitably gang players or organized crime affiliated elements, just as many were community-of-interest members, victims, and law enforcement investigators. My interviews were conducted in very different venues and contingent on a variety of factors, which heavily influenced how the research would proceed. These variables included, but were not limited exclusively to, informant availability, comfort levels, issues of personal safety, and sometimes just the convenience of those involved. Some interviews were conducted within the correctional system with both gang informants and players awaiting trial, while other interviews were with those who were already sentenced through the courts and were now serving prison time. In the correctional institutional setting in particular, there exists little doubt in my mind that being of the female gender was of immense advantage. Those I requested interviews with—both inside the correctional system and later on the outside—appeared to be much more likely to speak with me when advised that I was female: perhaps because of a gender dynamic, but also because of their being very conscious of perceptions among their peers. As explained by one of the incarcerated informants I spoke with, he was willing to talk to me because I was female and "It's not like I'm talking to the police". After having made introductions through the proper access channels and having asked to speak with this informant for a book I was writing—at that time a Master's thesis—this informant later explained to me that most of the other inmates would think I was his probation/parole worker or a social worker liaising between him and his family on the outside. Gender indeed proved to be an immeasurable advantage, particularly as it pertained to my ability to make notes for clarification and for the purposes of follow-up visitation.

The Ethnographic Process

The findings contained in this study represent the culmination of intensive interviews with informants over a period of time that spanned 15 years; both during my career as a police officer and later after I had left the profession. At times over the protracted course of this research, I occupied the seemingly conflicting positions of anthropologist, researcher, and police officer; a multi-role pursuit that provided me with the opportunity to earn the trust of informants from very diverse backgrounds. While academic ethics precluded my ability to conduct formal research while simultaneously occupying my role as a police officer, my police investigative experience certainly helped to inform and structure future interview opportunities that I would later pursue in the lone capacity of an academic researcher, intimately familiar with policing. The research favored an unstructured interview approach that "cast the net wide" and proceeded based on the responses received from those being interviewed. This interview style was chosen for two reasons: First, it partially corrected for issues of intercultural communication by allowing me to assess what informants thought they heard me ask, and second, when no answer was forthcoming, it provided an opportunity to take a closer look at why a particular question might not have been answered. In other words, what informants chose not to answer carried with it its own potential for further investigation; particularly when others similarly connected to some aspect of gang activity, proved equally as reluctant to speak about an issue. My questions were selected in the general domain of what brought me to the informant with whom I was speaking: their identification as a gang player, a gang associate, a gang victim, a gang investigator, and others. These questions then provided a starting point for what, in many cases, would become thematic interviews over time. Because of the unstructured interview strategy I used, I suppose it could be said that I never formally interviewed anyone during this extended period of research. I began with open-ended questions and the informants' answers formed the basis of follow-up questions and ensuing conversation. In some instances, I taped what informants related to me, but only with their permission and only when I asked them to explain, from their perspective, specific situations or apparent contradictions in what others had shared. This particular strategy was limited to those I came to know well or for those whose insights into gang life were already well established through police investigations and the courts. This approach provided a check against my own observations and field notes, and provided me with an opportunity to follow-up with informants on areas of perceived contradiction or in need of elaboration. As I proceeded over the course of many interviews with gang participants in particular, I was always reminded of an observation made almost a half-century ago, as it pertained to researchers seeking to explain a social order while reconciling the constructs used by informants with models used by outsiders:

> The scientific observer must take into account the common-sense constructs employed by the actor in everyday life if he is to grasp the meanings that will be assigned by the actor to his questions, regardless of the form in which they are presented to the actor (Cicourel 1964, p. 61).

Methodology

The methodology pursued during the times I "stepped out" of active policing for the purposes of this research, also utilized the long-standing ethnographic technique of participant observation, wherein I witnessed *in situ* instances of protection extortions and police "take downs" of suspected gang players. At other times,

I found myself engaged in participatory action research with community stake-holders, specifically those on the receiving end of protection and extortion rackets. And while much of this research was conducted during my career as a police officer, my informant interviews were done exclusively outside my policing jurisdiction, until such time as I left the policing profession for good. When I closed my policing career of 25 years, only then did I speak with gang informants from within my former policing jurisdiction; many now introduced by community members with whom I had liaised for many years prior. The rapport that had been established with these community conduits could now be best described as occurring between two interested stakeholders both looking to disrupt and forestall future gang violence: one entity participating from the perspective of building community awareness and capacity, and myself grappling to understand the structure and organization of twenty-first century street gangs which were increasingly morphing into both fluid and mobile criminal enterprise.

As a researcher engaged in an ethnographic pursuit informed by the divergent perspectives of police officer and anthropologist, I embarked on two additional anthropological traditions while conducting this protracted undertaking: The methodological pursuit of situational analysis, and the methodological/theoretical paradigm of social network analysis. Interviews conducted with gang informants about specific gang activities were particularly well served by situational analysis; a technique that provided an opportunity to examine past social interactions among gang players as a dynamic process of decision-making at the level of street gang leaders. Within a plurality of relations, street gang leaders made decisions con-cerning what social network links to activate, what links to respond to, and what links would remain dormant. During this decision making process, they shared with this researcher both the sources and destinations of their information flow and described how they safeguarded against any constraints that might impact on that information flow among those they preferentially activated.

The methodological and theoretical paradigm of social network analysis was found to be particularly well suited to the urban context, where it is acknowledged that for most individuals, no single group encapsulates all of one's activities. Rather, fields of interaction are seen to arise from where the actor-centred refer-ent—in my research street gang leaders—lived, worked, or played. The social network models included for discussion in this study represent those that most closely approximate the explanations and insights provided by those who were known street gang leaders, players, and, in one instance, a high-ranking organized crime figure. The rationale for selecting these models was provided by embarking on multi-sited and multi-timed informant interviews which both identified and supported their use.

In sum, what follows is information shared by informants during an interview process that spanned two decades—supported by police investigative findings and insights and corroborated by community of interest members and other victim stakeholders—that have collectively informed the definitions of "new-age" gangs, organized crime, and the "action-set", proposed by this author.

It has been said that "It is the wearer of the shoe that knows best where it pinches."[1]

The personal interview communications that have been selected for inclusion within this text depict, in my mind, the common-sense approach to gang activity shared by informants; both those who have either worn or felt the imprint of gang "shoes", and those who, to a lesser or greater extent, came to experience where gang life ultimately "pinched".

Reference

Cicourel, A. V. (1964). *Method and Measurement in Sociology*. New York: The Free Press.

---

[1] English proverb or adage of ambiguous authorship.

Contents

Chapter 1
Introduction to "New-Age" Gangs

The question of criminal street gangs in the North American context has become particularly confusing, as the media, law enforcement, and government agencies have tended to apply the term "street gangs" to highly organized criminal enterprises and loosely structured youth groups alike.

In contrast to the pattern of street gangs known from studies conducted on occidental gangs in the United States, "new-age" gangs[1] have tended to appear particularly unstructured. There exists little or no evidence of role differentiation; membership changes constantly; members have not shown any propensity to adopt common modes of dress; and the gangs have not typically claimed geographic or territorial "turf". In short, these gangs are not fitting neatly into the established pattern of either organized crime groups or geographically-anchored territorial-based street gangs.

While describing new-age street gangs in general is a difficult task owing to their seemingly unstructured nature, one characteristic does however, appear to be a constant and that is their remarkable fluidity. I use the term "fluid" to denote the loosely organized make-up of these street gangs and the interchangeable make-up of their members, who are better conceived of as "players"; a word that implies a configuration analogous to sports teams where individuals are mobilized and see action based on a leader-centred decision maker and elements of skill.

In contrast to their long-standing occidental gang counterparts with a fixed membership, new-age gang "players" are loyal only to the money to be made and when the money source runs dry, they are free to leave the street gang leader they are following and attempt to follow[2] another street gang leader. It is this dimension of fluidity among those involved—as mobilized through the street gang leader—that is best reflected by the term "players"; a term that this text will use in

---

[1] The term 'new-age' gangs is being applied to street gangs that have evolved on the North American scene over the past 15 years and have increasingly exhibited the dimensions of fluidity among participants and mobility across geographic jurisdictions.

[2] The term "follow" is an insider or *emic* terminology used by street gang leaders to reference organized crime affiliation. It is similarly used to reference street gang 'players' who are preferentially mobilized by a street gang leader and are referred to as that leader's 'following'.

C. E. Prowse, *Defining Street Gangs in the 21st Century*, SpringerBriefs in Criminology,
DOI: 10.1007/978-1-4614-4307-0_1, © The Author(s) 2012

preference to the term street gang "member". For clarity however, the term street gang "member" will be used on occasion as it applies to street gangs modeled in a paradigm of fixed membership and geographic anchorage or when reference is made to authors who have favored its use.

Associated with new-age gang structural fluidity is an equally significant geographic mobility which has hindered the attempts of law enforcement agencies to deal with street gangs modeled in the new-age paradigm; a model which paradoxically, does not appear to have diminished the intensity of personal bonds formed between the gang players. Today's gang leaders utilize networks of personnel that reach transnationally; a personnel reservoir with many members moving frequently between the criminal underworlds of Los Angeles, San Francisco, New York, Boston, and the major Canadian centres of Montreal, Ottawa, Toronto, Calgary, Edmonton, and Vancouver. Gang players utilize criminal connections made in stop-over points en route to their present location, and travel extensively throughout North America for both social and criminal reasons. As far back as 1990, the RCMP in Canada reported that street gang members operating between Montreal, Ottawa, and Toronto collectively defined the primary Southern Ontario corridor utilized by street gangs for criminal purposes in Canada and the United States. This observation became particularly manifest as a result of a 1991 arrest in Toronto of the fugitive leader of the notorious New York and Boston based "Born to Kill" gang—among the first to exhibit new-age gang structure. The incident as captured in Text Box 1 most vividly revealed the extraordinary mobility and fluidity which very early characterized new-age street gang activity.

Text Box 1

In 1990, a Calgary jeweller was robbed of over one-half million dollars in gold and diamonds by six young males during an incident that lasted for a matter of minutes and was executed with precision timing. All of the six subjects were later determined to be residents of the United States: three from Boston, two from Los Angeles, and one from New York; all associated to the then infamous Born to Kill gang.

A year later in Toronto, an escalation in gang-related violence would lead to the 1991 arrest of the fugitive leader of the New York and Boston-based Born to Kill gang. As a fugitive of the United States, the street gang leader operated from a base in Toronto; to avoid attention and elude police investigators, he utilized members of his American-based gang to carry out his criminal undertakings.

A joint forces operation by police agencies in Toronto, Calgary, and Montreal, along with police sources in the United States, later revealed that "mix and match" combinations of Born to Kill gang members were responsible for violent criminal activity in Toronto, Calgary, Edmonton, Atlantic City, New York, and New Jersey, in addition to numerous acts of cross-border smuggling involving property and firearms. At the time of his arrest in Toronto, police

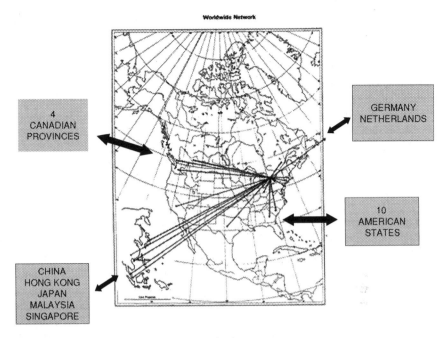

Map 1.1   Worldwide network of street gang leader

investigations revealed that the fugitive Born to Kill street gang leader had regular contact with a worldwide network of gang members and criminal associates located in China, Hong Kong, Japan, Malaysia, Singapore, West Germany, ten American states, and four Canadian provinces.

Map 1.1 depicts the worldwide network of gang players and associates mobilized by this particular street gang leader, as revealed during police investigations.

Toward an Operational Definition of "Gang"

The word "gang" may at first glance appear to beg a straightforward definition, however, since Thrasher's (1927) seminal work in the area, there has never existed a consensus among social scientists as to exactly what constitutes a gang. Today, defining a gang remains a source of vexation and, as attempts continue, they do so for the purpose of circumscribing a cluster of behaviors, characteristics, and activities that serve both academic endeavor and criminal justice accountability. Intervention, enforcement, and deterrence efforts are all furthered when a nebulous concept is made operationally tangible, which, in part, has accounted for both the diversity exhibited among gang definitions and the differing agendas held by those attempting such definitions.[3] Closely associated with the inherent difficulty of defining what constitutes a gang however, is that like the definitions themselves, gang structure varies. Today, new-age gangs are increasingly reflecting a social structure that facilitates 'business' by capitalizing on networks of associates built from established patterns of kinship, trade, and shared experience; not alike multinational ventures that seek to align their business operations with associations on the ground. In short, while the definitional proclivity continues to coalesce around a cluster of characteristics that support a structure, that structure has increasingly evolved from a fixed criminal membership to a mobile network of gang 'players' pursuing criminal opportunity.

One of the first documented references made to networks associated to street gangs was in reference to the criminal activities of ethnic-Vietnamese gangs and their tradition of preying almost exclusively on their countrymen (Gross 1989). The extraordinary mobility attached to these criminal groups in search of criminal activity, was a characteristic that was attributed to the tradition of large extended families found within Vietnamese culture. While first observed in the Orange County area of Southern California among the ethnic-Vietnamese community, this pattern of criminal participation has now become a widespread organizational phenomenon at the level of street gangs. In the absence of an organizationally closed gang structure, networks based on patronage provide a structural continuity to an otherwise seemingly unstructured pattern of gang activity.

In an attempt to account for the mobile structure first documented among ethnic-Vietnamese gangs of the day, Badey (1988) developed a comprehensive gang typology which focused exclusively on structure and organization. Utilizing his 20 years of policing experience in Arlington, Virginia, he divided street gangs into three types:

Formal Gangs

Formal gangs are those which have a definitive leader, a solid core of reliable and available members, and a geographical area and/or criminal activity under their control.

Informal Gangs

Informal gangs are by comparison to formal ones, new, loosely organized, and less focused. They often have a charismatic individual in his late twenties to mid-thirties who strives to establish himself as the leader. ... The fluctuation in membership size and the spread of membership ages are probably the two most important blockages toward their building of a more dynamic and ongoing organization. ... [and] denies them the ability to control a turf and/or specific criminal activity.

---

[3] Criminal justice practitioners and academics alike have emphasized different criteria in defining what constitutes a "gang". Wortley (2010) suggests that the various criteria that have been used coalesce around the following: age, group name, group symbols/insignia, territory, group organization, number of members, stability over time, gang rules, initiation rituals, street orientation, crime, violence, shared ethnic or racial background.

Casual Gangs

Casual gangs are thought of as groups of persons, mostly male, who habitually band together. They are, for the most part, leaderless and make their decisions to commit crimes by mutual discussion and agreement. They are freelancers who target their victims because of the victim's perceived wealth and availability. Sometimes, they will leave their home turf for distant locations to attack victims at the request of the leaders of formal gangs.

This text will present an alternative paradigm for interpretation and suggest that Badey's typology of more than 20 years ago very closely resembles new-age gangs in three phases of development or stability: **formal gangs** which exhibit the dimensions of mobility and a fluidity of "reliable and available members" resemble what this author has chosen to term "new-age" gangs with an identifiable leader who has affiliation with organized crime; **informal gangs** closely mirror a 'new-age' gang in the process of structuring with an emerging leader without a secure financial flow; and lastly, **casual gangs** are reminiscent of a destabilized and leaderless 'new-age' gang that has resorted to freelancing to meet expenses.

Vigil and Yun (1990) similarly researched the "new look" of the emerging ethnic-Vietnamese gang phenomenon in Southern California and proposed that delinquency among these youth was caused by social disorganization borne of the refugee experience. These authors attributed the mobility associated with their criminal activity to their "tenuous adjustment" to relocation which in turn "contributes to a fluid, mobile method of acquiring quick, ready cash." Drawing comparisons to established street gangs in the United States, these authors further observed that:

Juxtaposed to African-American and Chicano gangs, in these Vietnamese youth gangs there is little interest in territorial considerations, and the signs and rituals of graffiti and initiation are played down, if not absent. (1990:162)

Vigil and Yun's work underscores the importance of historical antecedents in the formation of gangs, and characterizes Vietnamese gang activity as "a quick fix to a fragmented, disjointed history" (1990:162). A study conducted a decade later in the greater Vancouver area in British Columbia, Canada, reached a similar conclusion as it pertained to immigrant youth (Gordon 2000). But while a "fragmented disjointed history" of truncated family networks may have been the catalyst for mobility in the quest for ready cash, this text will argue that the structure and organization of new-age gangs today is much more a result of collectivist cultural orientations that likewise emphasize pre-existing relationships and, by so doing, capitalize on transnational—and indeed transcontinental—social networks or "global ethnoscapes" (Appadurai 2000) that facilitate, and indeed favor, economic or commodity-based "turf".

Before proceeding, it is necessary to "wade through" the terminological baggage that has accumulated in the literature, in an attempt to separate "street gangs" from what have been described as "wannabe groups" or other "criminal groups". Using a typology developed by Gordon (2000) the following are characteristics associated with these terminological distinctions:

Criminal Groups

Small cluster of friends who band together, usually for a short period of time (no more than 1 year) to commit crime primarily for financial gain. They can be composed of young people and/or young, and not so young, adults and may be mistakenly, or carelessly, referred to as a gang.

Wannabe Groups

Young people who band together in a loosely structured group primarily to engage in spontaneous social activity and exciting, impulsive, criminal activity including collective violence against other groups of youths. A wannabe group will be highly visible and its members will boast about their "gang" involvement because they want to be seen by others as gang members.

Street Gangs

Groups of young people and young adults who band together to form a semistructured organization the primary purpose of which is to engage in planned and profitable criminal behavior or organized violence against rival street gangs.

The relevance of this typology rests with its attempt to differentiate between groups of individuals exhibiting varying degrees of structure, organization, duration, and collective identity; all of which have been loosely included under the rubric of "gang" at one time or another. This is not to suggest, that in particular contexts there has not existed a need for gang definitions to demonstrate flexibility, but rather to reinforce the great diversity associated with the phenomenon of collective criminality that has been variously captured by the word "gang".

Comparing definitions drawn from many diverse sources, the term "street gang" has been generally applied—by academics and practitioners alike—to those groups whose identity is shaped by a cluster of characteristics that preferentially emphasize or include the following:

1. Age range consisting of young adults and/or adults;
2. Has a name or identifiable leadership or structure;
3. Controls a geographic, economic, or criminal enterprise "turf";
4. Has a sustained or regular affiliation between those involved;
5. Engages in criminal activity which may include violence.

And, while both new-age gangs and those modelled in the long-standing North American model share elements of these characteristics, what differentiates the two gang paradigms is where the emphasis is placed and how enduring the role structure. While this is a discussion that will be fully developed in Chap. 3, it is necessary to emphasize at this juncture, that while new-age gangs do have an identifiable leader, the gang itself does not share an enduring membership structure. New-age gangs are mobilized based on relationship, not through identifiable enduring roles. Similarly, due to their fluid and mobile organization they do not emphasize geographic turf, but rather, are predicated on economic and commodity-based turf; a characteristic that breaks them free of geographic anchorage and a fixed membership structure. It is this characteristic of mobility across jurisdictions

<u>Occidental Gangs</u>   <u>"New-age" Gangs</u>

Gang members   Gang "players"

Fixed membership   Fluid participation

Geographic anchorage   Geographic mobility

Geographic "turf"   Commodity-based "turf"

Gang name   Gang name variable

Gang paraphernalia   No gang paraphernalia

Fig. 1.1 Occidental gangs and "new-age" gangs

in particular, that fuels encroachment and brings them into conflict with other street gangs modeled in the paradigm of geographic anchorage. Further elaboration on the dimensions of fluidity and mobility will be the focus of discussion in Chap. 3 however, for the purposes of elaboration, Fig. 1.1 dichotomizes between occidental street gangs and new-age street gangs.

Previous work shared by this author within the international law enforcement community, advocated for the application of social network theory to emergent street gangs whose organization was predicated on "fluidity and mobility as instruments of organization" (Prowse 1996). More recently, the Criminal Intelligence Service Canada has expanded their definition of "street gang" to include both descriptors of gangs modeled in the occidental paradigm, as well as a paradigm of street gang organization more in alignment with the relationship-based fluidity of a social network model:

> Some common characteristics among street gangs include specific gang identifiers and paraphernalia, a common name or identifying sign or symbol, induction rituals and a rigid or loose code relating to the conduct and duty of members and associates. ... Further, some street gangs are based on familial relations or friendships while others are hierarchical in nature with multiple cells and more complex networks. (CISC 2010, p. 19)

In both Canada and the United States, definitions of street gangs have placed an emphasis on what academics have referred to as gang "definers"[4] (Klein et al. 2006); those elements intended to separate gang criminality from that of random group criminality. The following represent operational definitions of "street gang" used in Canada and the United States respectively:

---

[4] "Definers" characterize a group as a gang based on specified gang definitional criteria; "descriptors" are characteristics specific to individual gangs and distinguish between the gangs, for example, gang names, symbols, or colors.

A street gang is a more or less structured group of adolescents, young adults and/or adults who use intimidation and violence to commit criminal acts on a regular basis, in order to obtain power and recognition and/or control specific areas of criminal activities (Canadian Centre for Justice Statistics 2008)

A criminal street gang is an ongoing group, club, organization or association of five or more persons formed for the purpose of committing a violent crime or drug offence, with members that have engaged, within the past five years, in a continuing series of violent crimes or drug law violations that affect interstate or foreign commerce (United States [Criminal] Code, s.521).

In both of the operational definitions above, an emphasis is placed on "definers" that include durability ("structured" or "ongoing"), a group identity shaped by "criminality" and, by implication, a street level orientation. In the Canadian context, the criminal street gang usage definition above finds inclusion under the provisions of the Canadian _Criminal Code_ s. 467.1 as a "criminal organization":

"Criminal Organization" means a group, however organized, that

a. is composed of three or more persons in or outside of Canada; and
b. has as one of its main purposes or main activities the facilitation or commission of one or more serious offences that, if committed, would likely result in the direct or indirect receipt of a material benefit, including a financial benefit, by the group or by any of the persons who constitute the group.

It does not include a group of persons that forms randomly for the immediate commission of a single offence.

The above definition however, is much broader than that used by the Canadian Centre for Justice Statistics and does not stipulate how enduring a "group" must be—only that it not be "immediate"—nor does it require the identification of an internal structure or organization. The definitions adopted by both the Canadian _Criminal Code_ and the _United States [Criminal] Code_ appear sufficiently broad to capture the characteristics increasingly exhibited by new-age gangs.

New-Age Gangs

In this text, interview data that now spans two decades has been used to gain analytical purchase on what increasingly presents as an alternative paradigm to occidental street gang organization and structure: new-age gangs. For the purposes of ensuing discussion, the term 'new-age' street gang will be introduced within the context of a criminal organizational hierarchy that reflects a three-tiered typology. The term "criminal organization" will be applied only in the context of the organized crime level and the new-age street gang level; in other words, it excludes the action-set level. Because the following represents a typology of criminal participation, violence in the pursuit of illegal enterprise, is implied as a inevitable ingredient to greater or lesser extents.

Organized Crime Group

A close-knit, geographically anchored group of enduring criminal associations, engaged in low-risk and high-gain criminal enterprise while also operating in the legal marketplace.

New-Age Gangs

A loose-knit and fluid group of associates who comprise a subset of a street gang leader's enduring social network and who are preferentially activated in the commission of street-based criminal activity through that street gang leader. A gang identity need not form part of their collective self-identification.

Action-Set

An unorganized and generally youthful (under 18 years) collective of potential criminal participants, known to the street gang leader through a social network of relations. Street gang participation is peripheral and on an *ad hoc* basis; it does not form part of their self-identification.

What needs to be emphasized pursuant to the above definitional typology however, is that at both the new-age gang and action-set levels, involvement in the criminal lifestyle is but only one dimension of the activities shared by those involved. Both the street gang players and the action-set participants are drawn from a wider set of social relations that comprise a street gang leader's personal network. By contrast, the organized crime group operates exclusively among other trusted career criminals and are primarily engaged in illegal enterprise.

The fluidity and mobility exhibited by new-age gangs is a feature of organization, not structural continuity. Structural continuity implies a state, whereby there are roles to be filled that will endure beyond those occupying the roles. This does not imply however, that new-age street gangs lack structure; what they lack is structural continuity that manifests as positions within the traditional or occidental paradigm of street gangs. While it may seem inherently contradictory to describe the participants as "players" while simultaneously implying a structure, this distinction rests with the observation that gang players are mobilized from a street gang leader's personal network of relations. It is this network of relationships that provides a structural continuity through its preferential activation of players.

References

Appadurai, A. (2000). Grassroots globalization and the research imagination. *Public Culture*, *12*(1), 1–19.

Badey, J. R. (1988). *Dragons and tigers*. Loomis: Palmer enterprises.

Canadian Centre for Justice Statistics. (2008). *Uniform crime reporting incident-based survey: CCJS reporting manuel*. Ottawa: Statistics Canada.

Criminal Intelligence Service Canada. (2010). *Annual Report on Organized Crime in Canada*. Ottawa: Director General, CISC.

Gordon, R.M. (2000). Criminal business organization, street gangs and 'wanna-be' groups: A vancouver perspective. *Canadian Journal of Criminology*, *42*(1), 39–60.

Gross, G. (1989). The Vietnamese Crime Network. In M. Launer & J.E. Palenski (Eds.), *Crime and the new immigrants*, Springfield: Charles C.Thomas.

Klein, M., Weerman, F., & Thornberry, T. (2006). Street gang violence in europe. *European Journal of Criminology, 3*, 413–437.

Prowse, C. (1996). *Vietnamese criminal organizations: fluidity and mobility as instruments of organization*. Calgary: Calgary Police Service.

Thrasher, F. M. (1927). *The gang*. Chicago: University of Chicago Press.

Vigil, J.D. & Yun, S.C. (1990). Vietnamese youth gangs in southern california. In R. Huff (Ed.). *Gangs in America*, Newbury Park: Sage.

Wortley, S. (2010). *Identifying street gangs: definitional dilemmas and their policy implications*. Ottawa: Public Safety Canada.

Chapter 2
The Gang as a Network

Everything went through him [leader]. He controlled 'x' many people who only knew 'x' many people, whereas he [leader] was the key because he knows the whole thing [network]

While the dimensions of fluidity and mobility were first exhibited in the North American context years ago by ethnic-Vietnamese criminal organizations (Vigil and Yun 1990), they are no longer exclusive to them alone. Actually, what they exhibited over two decades ago has been increasingly adopted by other criminal enterprises, who have realized it advantageous to align their operational structure with their commodity flow. And, as "new-age" gangs continue to adopt a network structure that facilitates fluidity among participants and geographic mobility—and by so doing become a source of media attention and law enforcement vexation—it is anticipated that an awareness of social formations borne of necessity and shaped by cultural antecedents, will become increasingly essential.

Social Network Models

In order to secure analytical purchase of social formations, networks represent an empirically grounded model of social structure that grew out of an increasing awareness that spatial boundaries do not delimit social boundaries. The primary objective of analyzing an individual's social network then, is to be able to move beyond the constraints and boundaries imposed by a spatial locale. In short, the social environment that characterizes the urban context is best conceived of as the network of actual social relationships maintained, regardless of whether these are confined to a specific area or extend well beyond its boundaries (Bott 1955).

Social network analysis adopts an ego-centred perspective that focuses on how individuals are connected to others, and recognizes—that for most people—there is no single group that encapsulates their daily activities.

Interview with a former gang player who is referencing the street gang leader he followed.

C. E. Prowse, *Defining Street Gangs in the 21st Century*, SpringerBriefs in Criminology, DOI: 10.1007/978-1-4614-4307-0_2, © The Author(s) 2012

The approach taken in this text will focus on the network as a process for the mobilization of action, rather than on the quantification of network characteristics; the latter representing a sociometric path that has emerged since the origins of network analysis in ethnography, and which some suggest "directs attention exclusively to the overall structure of network ties while suppressing consideration of their substantive content" (Emirbayer and Goodwin 1994, p. 1440). As a paradigm from which explanations surrounding social action can be extracted from patterns of relationships, network analysis dismisses explanations of "social behaviour as the result of individuals' common possession of attributes and norms rather than as a result of their involvement in structured social relations" (Wellman 1983, p. 165). In other words, if we are to account for how individuals come together for a common objective, it is essential that we look beyond the potentially shared attributes of age, gender, religion, social status, or ethnicity, and focus on the network of relationships within which they exist.

Unlike the long-standing occidental gang paradigm (see Fig. 1.1), new-age street gangs are not geographically anchored to an area; rather they are most often characterized by their extraordinary mobility and fluidity of gang composition. The mobility which characterizes their activities has tended to produce loose-knit networks which show little redundancy or overlap in connectedness among the network links. This has served to create a network of gang players where mediating links are of critical importance in determining gang structure and organization. To accomplish the examination of a network then, one cannot merely propose to indicate the links between people, as this is adequately described by the word "relationship". Rather, it is necessary to document further linkages to the links themselves or risk failing to account for much of the social context within which decisions are made. Accomplishing this requires reference to contextual social network models which provide a framework for analyzing associations between individuals, and that flow from established relationships. Broadly speaking, these network models can be generalized into three approaches; each of them uniquely emphasizing Boissevain's "friends of friends" typology that embodies the element of trust, so critical to the survival of new-age gangs.

In order to describe phenomenon shared by new-age gang players and informants over the course of an extended period of research, I have borrowed models from social network analysis. Each of the analytic models that follow distinguishes between patterns of social relationships that allow us to differentiate between enduring association and objective-activated joint activity. The coalitions model describes new-age gang formation and mobilization; the network-set model describes the potential for rival gangs to be created; and the action-set model provides a prototype for how action-set participants are recruited.

The Network-Set Model[1]

In this model, social relationships exist in an unbounded network of ego-centred "sets" that lack either leadership or a coordinating organization. Any person is believed to have relations with a number of people, who in turn are linked to others; however, the prevailing characteristic of association to the network requires that members share an underlying bond such as kinship, economics, or a 'community of interest'. The set is ego-centred in that it is focused on an individual, and consists of the people classified by ego according to a specific criterion. Following through on the kinship analogy, kinship linkages would represent the network, and all those classified as "brothers" would form the set. These people therefore form only part of the network—that part which ego recognizes as being contained in the set in some specifiable context. Barnes conceives of the network as being the basis for sets, rather than as a means of describing them. It is this intrinsic ability to view the network as a constellation of sets built on dyadic relationships, that in turn allows us to conceive of it as a reservoir of ego-centred networks each equally possessing the ability to structure and rival existing or prevailing ego-centred networks that have already established a coordinating leadership.

The Action-Set Model[2]

A related way in which personal networks have been conceived has been characterized as the "action-set" model. Under this paradigm, a certain number of linkages which already exist in the total network of a 'community of interest' may be mobilized for a specific and limited purpose. This type of network is called the action-set, and its mobilization implies some transaction between an "ego" or reference point, and the persons in the action-set. The individuals mobilized in an action-set may be activated through a sequence of leader-centred connections, or they may be recruited directly by the street gang leader through a dyadic relationship. An action-set therefore, is delineated in terms of the specific transaction which brings it into being, making the mobilization of individuals in this position contingent on the activation of the gang player through whom they were contacted. When individuals in the action-set exist through a series of contexts of activity, without any formal basis for membership, they are best conceived of as "quasi-groups" that represent a pool of potential gang players or recruits who represent "aggregates or portions of the community which have no recognizable

---

[1] The network-set model presented here was first proposed by Barnes (1972).

[2] The term action-set was first attributed to Van Velzen (1971), however, it is being applied in this text consistent with Mayer's (1978) typology which focuses on its activation.

structure, but whose members have certain interests or modes of behaviour in common, which may at any time lead them to form themselves into definite groups" (Ginsberg 1934, p. 40). This group would be somewhat analogous to what authors have described as "youth groups": small clusters of youth who "hang out" together in public places (Gordon 2000).

The Coalitions Model[3]

The coalitions model views members of ego's personal network who are preferentially mobilized for a specific purpose or goal-oriented criminal activity, as coalitions. In contrast to the action-set model, this model conceives of coalitions as existing only until the goal is attained, at which time the members of the coalition cease to be linked by a common pattern of action and re-enter the category of ego's personal network of potential players. The parties to the coalition retain their unique individual identity which is not replaced by a group identity, nor are their individual commitments subsumed to a uniform and group-focused set of expectations. The coalition can be thought of as a consciously constructed social entity in the sense that the linkages activated and maintained within the group have an ego-centred leader. This leader-centred social network has been conceived of in the literature as an "interest coalition" (Van Velzen 1971) because it is brought into being by that leader to satisfy a specific undertaking. As such, mobilization can be conceived of as a series of transactional linkages between a leader and his followers; followers who are not necessarily connected or known to one another. Police intelligence reports have referred to this type of structure as "cells", noting that "a cell-based structure does not mean that there are no leaders within the group" (CISC 2005, p. 6). I would argue that the cells being referenced by law enforcement are actually a combination of two phenomena: independent coalitions with an identifiable street gang leader and, a "mix and match" configuration of gang players within an individual coalition as preferentially mobilized through the street gang leader. It is worthy of note that the coalitions model is not inconsistent with Barnes's network-set model; indeed coalition members are drawn from sets within ego's personal network. The difference is realized when one of the ego-centred networks preferentially mobilizes members from within their larger network of relations for an indeterminate period of time, at which point we can allow our terminology to reflect this change in structure and use the term "coalition". A coalition has a mobilizing and coordinating leadership that draws on network-sets.

---

[3] The coalitions model presented here was first proposed by Boissevain (1971).

"New-Age" Gang Networks

As each of the above models suggest, one cannot totally separate personal, social, and goal-oriented activities when seeking to establish a network of trusted associates. All possible and potentially relevant social dimensions have to be considered, which necessitates a shift in focus from individual gang 'players' to networks of relationships.

The unit of analysis critical to analyzing new-age gang structure is the nature of the relationship. All of the models presented focus on ego-centred relationships that have been brought about by a pattern of interaction that reflects what has been described as the "live, work, or play" site (Brantingham and Brantingham 1993): kinship ties, "friends of friends", employment, community-of-interest participation, or communication links activated through these associations. While these relationship-based network models serve to illuminate patterns of association that may exist, it is worth emphasizing that personal attributes such as sex, age, language, and ethnicity—while perhaps shared by those in the relationship—do not form the basis of that relationship (Prowse 1993). This observation will be discussed to a greater extent in Chap. 5.

The fluid dimension of gang players in an ever-increasingly connected world, reinforces what each of the included models emphasizes: primacy rests within a plurality of relationships that occur across ego-centred networks. A network 'anchored' around a particular member of the group can be conceived of as ego-centred because it represents social relationships of all kinds. Partial networks based on relationships borne of kinship obligations, work or school relationships, or friendship ties, are activated from the leader's ego-centred network and are focused around particular types of activities. As such, social relationships based on ascriptive characteristics such as age, sex, language, ethnicity, cannot be separated from economic pursuits. The strength of the commitment to the activity then—criminal or otherwise—tends to be influenced by the multiplexity of the relationship: those based on a number of commonalities are stronger because they exist across different venues of intersection such as those represented by the "live, work, or play" paradigm; an observation made many years earlier by the Manchester school of network theorists (Gluckman 1967).

Relationships based on social solidarity and diffuse obligations are structured by a history of interaction between the members of an ego-centred network, however because networks facilitate function, it should not be assumed that they are devoid of the search for individual advantage. From the standpoint of a gang leader about to activate elements of his network, he needs to know whether those he activates can be trusted, since even kin-based networks can be characterized by diffuse solidarity and moral obligation. As such, they are no less susceptible to the pursuit of individual advantage than any others (Stack 1974). A leader's security is not ensured by a loyalty commitment from his players, but rather his security is assured by the effectiveness of the network in ensuring the desired objective is attained.

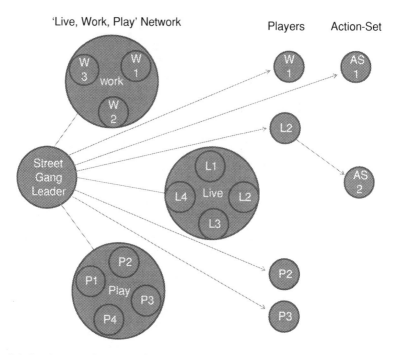

Fig. 2.1 Leader-centred network of potential gang "players"

In urban settings in particular, where relationships are specially developed based on points of articulation that cluster around where one lives, has commitments, or associates, personal relationships arising from these sites are frequently single-stranded and often rarely endure past the interaction that brought them into being. By contrast, multi-stranded relationships drawn from network-sets that include kinship, can extend the geographic range of ego's network, and endure independently past the cessation of a particular criminal undertaking. This observation has been termed "labour market kinship" (Harris 1990); a diminishing phenomenon long-associated with the modernity of early-industrial societies, and one which has become increasingly foreign in today's postmodern Western society. However, as theorists have argued, not all aspects of today's industrial-based societies conform to modernity nor do all facets of contemporary societies conform to post-modernism (Harris 1990). In short, while gang players are drawn from a street gang leader's personal network, it is important to clarify that while the interplay between his personal network and economic pursuits may become a characteristic of each, they are not the defining characteristic. Specific personal relationships that utilize kinship may be used to further economics, and specific economic relationships may be furthered on the basis of personal ties, but each of these occurs as a result of pre-existing relationships formed in distinct spheres of interaction. Relationships arising out of established kinship ties, shared experience, and established migration and/or trade patterns, collectively comprise associations in space as otherwise described as "global ethnoscapes" (Appadurai 2000). The mobilization of these connections occurs then, in the context of both moral economies necessitating financial obligation to family in the form of remittances and/or social economies to satisfy personal benefit and economic "tributes". In short, the application of social network analysis provides an opportunity to see new-age gang players—and in particular the leader position—as ethnographic subjects of study within the context of transactional linkages preferentially activated and mobilized to satisfy perceived need and/or want. By so doing, the definition of "new-age" street gangs put forward in this text reflects a paradigm shift from definitions currently in use; this author proposes that rather than focusing on the characteristics of the group collective to define a "gang",[4] perhaps the time has come to focus on the characteristics of a leader-centred relationship-based network of gang "players" (Fig. 2.1).

References

Appadurai, A. (2000). Grassroots globalization and the research imagination. *Public Culture, 12*(1), 1–19.

Barnes, J. A. (1972). *Social networks. Addison-Wesley module in anthropology 26*. Phillipines: Addison-Wesley.

Boissevain, J. (1971). Second thoughts on quasi-groups, categories and coalitions. *Man, 6*, 468–472.

Bott, E. (1955). Urban families: Conjugal roles and social networks. *Human Relations, 8*(4), 345–384.

Brantingham, P., & Brantingham, P. (1993). Environment, routine, and situation: Toward a pattern theory of crime. In R. Clarke & M. Felson (Eds.), *Routine activity and rational choice: Advances in criminological theory* (Vol. 5). New Brunswick, NJ: Transaction Publishers.

Criminal Intelligence Service Canada. (2005). *2005 Annual report on organized crime in Canada*. Ottawa: Director General, CISC.

Emirbayer, M., & Goodwin, J. (1994). Network analysis, culture, and the problem of agency. *American Journal of Sociology, 99*(6), 1411–1464.

Ginsberg, M. (1934). *Sociology*. London: Butterworth.

Gluckman, M. (1967). Introduction. In A. L. Epstein (Ed.), *The craft of social anthropology*. London: Social Science Paperbacks.

Gordon, R. M. (2000). Criminal business organization, street gangs and 'Wanna-Be' groups: A vancouver perspective. *Canadian Journal of Criminology, 42*, 39–60.

Harris, C. C. (1990). *Kinship*. Minneapolis: University of Minnesota.

Klein, M., Weerman, F., & Thornberry, T. (2006). Street gang violence in Europe. *European Journal of Criminology, 3*, 413–437.

Mayer, A. C. (1978). The significance of quasi-groups in the study of complex societies. In M. Banton (Ed.), *The social anthropology of complex societies*. London: Tavistock.

Prowse, C. E. (1993). A network analysis of Vietnamese criminal organizations. Unpublished Master's Thesis. University of Calgary, Canada.

---

[4] The characteristics being referenced would be consistent with what Klein et al. (2006) have termed gang "definers".

Stack, C. B. (1974). *All our kin: Strategies for survival in a black community.* New York: Harper & Row.

Van Velzen, H. U. E. (1971). Coalitions and network analysis. In J. Boissevain & J. C. Mitchell (Eds.), *Network analysis studies in human interaction.* The Hague: Mouton.

Vigil, J. D., & Yun, S. C. (1990). Vietnamese youth gangs in southern California. In R. Huff (Ed.), *Gangs in America.* Newbury Park: Sage.

Wellman, B. (1983). Network analysis: Some basic principles. In R. Collins (Ed.), *Sociological theory.* San Francisco: Jossey-Bass.

Chapter 3
From Fixed to Mobile; Members to Players

> *Q. Why do they call you the leader of a street gang?*
> *A. If they say I'm a gang leader, then I say to them: "What is my gang name?"*

A characteristic of many of the street gang players interviewed over the past 15 years was that gang activity was but one of the many activities this network of "friends of friends" shared in common. In actuality, those who participated within gang activity were drawn from those they already knew through a multiplex of relationships and associations. As such, ethnocultural alignment among the players involved in gang activity did exist, but only to the extent that the trust already established from pre-existing relationships provided a necessary ingredient for participation in criminal undertakings. What brought many of them together initially was a shared feeling of obligation to assist family members either at home or in another source country. A new-age street gang leader once explained, that despite his parents having never asked of him, he as their son knew that it was his "job" to look after them in their later years, however he had failed in that obligation. What this particular informant was referring to—in addition to the lengthy prison sentence he was currently serving—was a crack cocaine habit that had cost him upwards of $1,000 per week, and his inability to provide his refugee parents with the necessary funds to assist their relocation efforts.

Attachment and following a particular new-age street gang leader is not absolute by any means. At its simplest, a gang means making money, after which gang "players" are free to disassociate themselves from future involvement; follow other gang leaders; or themselves structure and rival existing leaders. Long-term gang participants frequently tire of following an established street gang leader and will often attempt to position themselves to preferentially rival for affiliation at the level of organized crime. Doing so however, inevitably results in outbreaks of violence—primarily directed at an affiliated gang leader's following—as a way of garnering power and itself a "ticket" to making money. Ultimately, the loyalty of gang players is primarily to the money to be made, and something gang leaders

---

This was a question posed by this author to a gang "player" who was generally acknowledged among police investigators and fellow gang participants as the leader.

C. E. Prowse, *Defining Street Gangs in the 21st Century*, SpringerBriefs in Criminology, DOI: 10.1007/978-1-4614-4307-0_3, © The Author(s) 2012

are acutely aware of. The sharing of knowledge by a gang leader with gang players on how to make money carries with it the risk of being undermined. As described by a former gang player:

> If the leader gets caught, the gang is quiet because there is no way to make money. If I was leader, I wouldn't tell the whole gang, the whole group, where to go to make money because I won't be leader no more.

Such an allegiance keeps a street gang leader in a constant position of vulnerability and under intense pressure to meet his payroll. If the street gang leader is "taken out" as a targeted attack, 'taken down' by police, or has no way to meet his payroll, that particular leader is finished and his following moves on should they choose to remain active. While new-age gang players frequently used the word "loyalty" to describe their involvement in gang activity, there exists an incongruity between what they describe to outsiders as "loyalty", and what is generally understood by the term. To understand the usage of the word as applied to participation in new-age street gangs, it should be interpreted only as a tie between the gang players involved and financial gain. Like power, loyalty is not inherent in a particular individual's personage, but rather, is an allegiance which exists as long as it remains financially viable. The insight offered by a former gang player who left the lifestyle by choice, demonstrates this observation:

> The loyalty is to money, not to the person. If I'm your follower, the only reason I follow you is because you can offer me money. If someone else offers me more, I will follow them because my loyalty is to make money. Everyone is out to make money and co-operation is good as long as that co-operation is profitable.

Although gang players are drawn from the gang leader's personal network of relations, it is necessary to understand that gang leaders activate players preferentially. In so doing, there are potential players wanting to make money that are not activated, which leaves them free to respond to other network links that they too possess and that in turn, carry the potential to provide them with an alternative opportunity to make money.

It is at this juncture that a clarification must be made between two structural levels within a criminal organization. In order to avoid confusion and ensure consistency during the ensuing discussion, I will designate those engaged in street gang activity as a distinct "street gangs" level, and designate any higher level of organization within the criminal organization as the "organized crime" level. The organized crime level will include down to the street gang leader, and when I refer to a "criminal organization" I am actually including both the organized crime level and an affiliated street gang leader's mobilized "following".[1]

While the term "criminal organization" has been loosely applied to unaffiliated criminal groups, street gangs, and organized crime structures alike, "criminal organization" is a term that will be used in the ensuing discussion to refer two

---

[1] The word "following" is an *emic* or insider terminology that is used to reference a new-age gang leader's preferentially activated players.

distinct levels of criminal sophistication: street gangs and organized crime; the distinction resting with the ability of each to pursue criminal enterprise as an enduring source of revenue.

Organized Crime Level

The organized crime level is characterized by a geographically anchored recognized leadership surrounded by a close-knit network of trusted criminal associates and a loose-knit network of worldwide connections. I describe this level within the structure as close-knit because there exists a redundancy among the connectedness between individuals occupying the positions within the structural framework; a framework that transcends those who occupy the positions within that structure.

"New-Age" Street Gang Level

In contrast to the organized crime level, the new-age street gang level is characterized by loose-knit networks of gang players following a street gang leader who has landed affiliation at the level of organized crime, and who exhibit a high degree of mobility in the commission of criminal acts. The mobility which characterizes this level within new-age criminal organizational structure is both a result of freelance activities as well as criminal activity directed by the organized crime level of the structure, which may necessitate the street gang players traveling to other jurisdictions in the commission of lucrative criminal undertakings. Once affiliated, street gang leaders are frequently loaned by the organized crime level to counterparts operating in other jurisdictions, and are expected to cooperate with gang leaders and players from other jurisdictions in the pursuit of particularly high-risk criminal activity. The street gang leader remains the key figure in gaining an analytical purchase on the structure of criminal organizations wherein they occupy a position of interface in the structural division between the organized crime level and street gang levels in a criminal organization.

Structural Interface

The existence of a structural and organization boundary between these two levels within a criminal organizational enterprise has been noted by researchers for over two decades in their attempts to define organized crime and street gangs.[2] Although operational definitions coalesce around common characteristics, their relevance lies with the structural boundary drawn between organized crime and street gangs; the criteria for distinction focused on both the organization of the individuals involved and the enduring structure that facilitates the degree of criminal sophistication associated to their activities.

While organized crime level members continue to receive money obtained through the proceeds of street crimes, it is well acknowledged that these earnings are laundered into legitimate business pursuits and property holdings. During an interview, an organized crime level informant revealed that organized crime leaders have a close-knit core group of people that they discuss "business" with and many others working for them. Those numbers would include all levels within the organized crime hierarchy and affiliated street gang leaders, however would not include those independently recruited by the street gang leaders as followers or players within their own street gang. What the organized crime following actually translates to, is a payroll of people each receiving a retainer from the organized crime level. This particular informant went on to explain how police "busts" actually fueled ensuing outbreaks of violence because when criminal business was interrupted, street gang leaders would engage in freelance activities—frequently extortion—to meet their payroll; an activity that inevitably encroached on the economics of other gangs maintaining geographic anchorage or "turf". The acknowledgment by an organized crime level figure of a payroll is a significant revelation because it speaks to an organizational structure with financial commitments. In turn, if the street gang leader is unable to meet his financial commitments, the loyalty shown to the leader by his followers is undermined, hence the need to resort to freelancing to meet expenses. As previously quoted, loyalty is not vested within the street gang leader, but within the money he can generate for those that "follow" him.

Associated with the organized crime level are a number of conduits who act as middle-men between the organized crime group and the street gang level. The freelance autonomy enjoyed by street gang players suggests that the geographically anchored position maintained by conduits represents a likely interface between the organized crime level and street gang level within a criminal organizational structure. The conduit position would include the property or commodity "fences", weapons suppliers, drug suppliers, and sex-trade suppliers, with whom the street gang leaders would deal directly. Conversations with a street gang leader who was sent to another jurisdiction as part of a widespread fraudulent credit card scheme, confirmed that he dealt primarily with a designated property "fence" who was his conduit to the organized crime group he followed, and to whom he turned over the proceeds for liquidation. The street gang leader position

---

[2] The work of Hagan (1983) was among the first to establish a definitional distinction; the existence of such a structural definitional boundary is now commonplace in the annual reports of national intelligence agencies .

presents a critical element in the structure of new-age street gangs if attempts to impact their activities are to be successful, because it is the position of street gang leader that interfaces with the lowest levels of organized crime: the street conduits. Street gang leaders receive direction from organized crime level conduits on how to handle their criminal undertakings: where to transport and/or distribute drugs, mule weapons, liquidate criminal proceeds; all so that they may receive their "cut" of the proceeds. That "cut" or the street gang leader's share of the criminal proceeds is in turn used to pay street gang players and any assisting associates. To place the profitability of gang player participation in context, police sources reveal that an initial $1,000 expenditure in cocaine can be converted to up to four times its amount in "crack", which can then be sold to street buyers at again 4–5 times its worth.[3] Affiliated street gangs share in this inflated return, which is now conservatively 15 times the worth of the initial purchase. It is this enhanced profit margin for those street gang leaders who are affiliated with organized crime that can fuel what appears to outsiders as seemingly sporadic outbreaks in violence between street gang leaders and their respective followings. Actually, these violent outbursts are generally preceded by a number of pre-incident indicators and hostilities discussed in Chap. 4. Figure 3.1 depicts the structural interface between the organized crime and street gang levels.

Characteristic to the street gang level is the autonomy they retain over their freelance "guns for hire" status, while simultaneously following an organized crime group. It is implicitly the street gang level which is referred to when the mobility and fluidity attached to new-age gangs are spoken of. In reality, every new-age street gang leader is the center of a plurality of relations and has the potential of activating a network of associates arising out of contacts cultivated while in the employ of organized crime.

So, at what point does a gang player aspire to become a street gang leader? The transition appears to rest on the ability of someone in the following to identify a source of predictable income and then, in turn, mobilize his own ego-centered network of trusted associates. The emerging street gang leader will assert control through his ability to meet a payroll, control the communication flow, and preferentially activate players. The importance of maintaining control over your network of contacts is emphasized to such an extent that all players mobilized for particular criminal undertakings are contacted by the street gang leader personally.

What became evident throughout interviews was that the criteria for recruitment and continued employment by the gang remained consistent up to the organized crime level of the criminal structure: the most ruthless, violent, or those who possess special skills within the action-set, are those who most readily land continued participation with the street gang.

An analysis of new-age street gang players revealed that they are closely intertwined with a street gang leader's personal network, having been drawn from

---

[3] Information provided during personal communication with police drug enforcement investigators, 2008.

associations made over time. For this reason, a leader's gang can be said to be ego-centered in that it exists because of him. Once a street gang leader has landed "work" or selected a target, he alone notifies each member of his street gang personally, as opposed to allowing the message to be conveyed between mobilized players. In turn, any secondary associates or action-set participants would be notified by the street gang player through which they are associated. Figure 3.2 depicts the "spoked pattern" of communication favored by street gang leaders in preference to a "circular pattern" of communication. The spoked pattern of communication is also employed for payment distribution to participants upon completion of their specific task. The loose-knit network exhibited by the street gang allows a leader to control the mobilization of his gang by controlling the information flow. The "spoked" communication pattern provides the street gang leader with the opportunity to exclude previous gang players or activate alternate players possessing special expertise. This pattern of communication also ensures that if any of the street gang players are intercepted or arrested, their knowledge of the gang's operations would be limited to what they had been told by the leader, and moreover their ability to impede the mobilization of the gang by interrupting the flow of information is rendered remote.

What is most significant when attempting to impact new-age gangs is to recognize that when affiliated, they become part of a criminal organizational structure with two very distinct levels of criminal sophistication. The organized crime level represents the geographically anchored hierarchy in the structure, characterized by a loose-knit network of worldwide associates and a redundancy in their connectedness. Expressed alternatively, the geographically anchored hierarchy are career criminals who know each other; a characteristic that lends both stability and continuity to this level of a criminal organizational structure. The street gang level of the criminal enterprise receives direction from the organized crime level in some activities but also freelance in other types of activities when the payroll is compromised; either because another street gang leader has been preferentially assigned a task or because a particular street gang leader has brought too much unwanted attention to his activities. Street gangs are responsible for carrying out high-risk and medium to low-gain activities, and are characterized by a highly mobile and loose-knit network known to, and mobilized through, the street gang leader.

It is critical to mention at this juncture a third level of organizational structure that is represented by what can be termed the "action-set" (Mayer 1978); a group which consists of generally young males under 18 years of age who are aspiring to become players in the street gangs' money-making activity. Participants at the action-set level can show isolated or regular peripheral involvement in the criminal activities of street gangs, however their participation is limited to criminal activities for which they have a special expertise and which do not involve participation with the regular players of the street gang. Individuals in the action-set can be considered to have achieved street gang player status when they are activated through a dyadic relationship with the street gang leader to actually participate with the street gang in the criminal undertaking, not merely as peripheral contributors. Although street gang players are the most frequent source for recruiting action-set participants, they

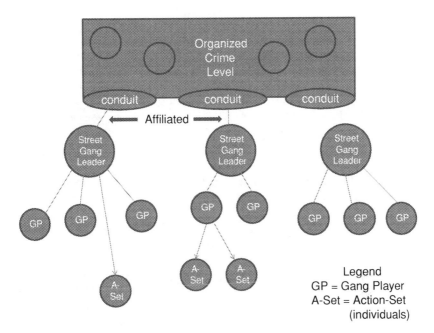

Fig. 3.1 Criminal organizational structure

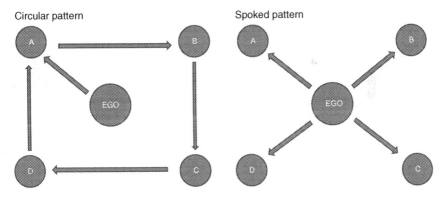

Fig. 3.2 Patterns of communication

can also be mobilized through a street gang leader's own network of relationships. When activated, action-set members further the activities of street gangs and for this reason, are described as a distinct level. Their activities are however, peripheral to, and in furtherance of, those of new-age street gangs. While they are being referenced as a distinct level of criminal activity, it is only for the purposes of recognizing their existence as an underage resource that is mobilized through the personal network of a street gang leader. Action-set participants who perform well may be eventually activated by street gang leaders as part of their following, just as successful street gang leaders are recruited to follow the organized crime level, should they prove valuable in their ability to generate income for this level of the criminal organization. The more violent or intimidating the street gang, the more likely they are to be successful in extracting or generating money for the organized crime level and, in so doing, street gang leaders gain recognition and possibly advancement within the criminal organizational structure. The appeal of violence and intimidation as they lead to power and money can be viewed as a formula for advancement within criminal organizations and can be depicted as

violence → power → money.

Unlike most occidental gangs modeled in the North American paradigm of geographic anchorage, new-age street gangs are characterized by their fluidity of gang membership and mobility across police jurisdictions in the pursuit of criminal activity and money. What must be understood however, is that these characteristics are reflective of a loose-knit criminal network as opposed to a close-knit geographically anchored street gang structure with a high degree of built-in connectedness among its gang members; a pattern of association that continues to characterize established occidental street gangs. The loose-knit network pattern observed at the new-age street gang level presents an unstructured *ad hoc* appearance, when in fact the street gang leader represents a distinct level of interface with a rigidly stratified organized crime structure which transcends those who occupy the positions within that structural framework. While this observation was first noted among Asian-based criminal organizational structures following transnational networks, it has been increasingly adopted by new-age gangs generally, for the advantages posed by a fluid and mobile structure. Police investigations are predicated on the repetition of a *modus operandi* [method of operation] that seeks to identify a commonality between offences that extends to suspect descriptions, and rely extensively on information from external sources. When the dimensions of fluidity among gang players and mobility across policing jurisdictions are deployed, there exists little doubt that police investigations are hampered as these long-standing avenues of investigation are compromised.

Investigating gangs modeled in the new-age paradigm can be made without reference to networks, however the interest in studying networks can be found in the insight it lends to understanding the connections affecting the social relations among the players. As a member of a network, every person can be seen as the center of a plurality of relations. Some of these are activated through contacts, while others remain inactive and dormant. To fulfill obligations and to pursue an individual's own ends, each person has to decide what network links to activate; what network links to respond to; what links to redefine; and which links to let fade away. The utility of examining personal networks rests with its ability to reveal if, in fact, there exists a coherent and persistent structural continuity; the basic strength of focusing on the identification of an organizational structure is that it can reveal the relationships that comprise that microcosm of a social system. By uncovering the structure of new-age gangs whose high-risk activities make them the most manifest representation of a criminal organization, we can trace both vertical and lateral flows of communication; identify sources and targets of information; and detect any structural constraints operating on that communication and resource flow. The utility of this type of approach to law enforcement agencies was recognized very early on by the then Director of the Federal Bureau of Investigation, who emphasized the need, particularly as it pertained to the structure of organized crime, to "attack the entire criminal enterprise rather than individual members" (Sessions 1991:13). While this particular quote referenced Asian-based criminal organizations, what set them apart at the time this observation was made, was their combination of geographic anchorage at the organized crime level and fluidity and mobility at the street gang level; together capitalizing on existing transnational and transcontinental networks to further the criminal organizational enterprise. The fluid and mobile nature of new age street gangs is very reminiscent of a collectivist social structure that favors relationship-based group-focused activities that endure only until the social action or objective is met.

This chapter began with a quote from a street gang player who was generally acknowledged among law enforcement and community sources as the leader of a new-age street gang. What was of particular interest however, was that despite him already having been convicted of many of the criminal charges laid, this individual remained reluctant to be recognized as the leader of a street gang. While it was never ascertained whether he objected to personally being identified as a gang 'leader' or merely preferred not be potentially implicated in charges associated with other gang players, what is known is that street gang participants—particularly those modeled in the new-age paradigm—are reluctant to adopt a gang name. Reasons for this are variable: some suggesting differing cultural meanings attached to the word 'gang'; some suggesting a legal awareness of the implications associated with being considered a "gang" participant; some suggesting that to forego a gang name provides an opportunity to operate in relative anonymity. What is known is that street gangs modeled in the new-age paradigm are, with increased frequency, either not adopting a name for their group or denying its existence. While the taking of names has been associated with increased attention from unwanted sources such as police, the media, and structuring rivals—and has certainly been a reason for street gang leaders being 'cut adrift' by the organized crime level—an equally significant reason for denying a gang name rests with an awareness of the potential legal implications for doing so. In the Canadian context, legislation enacted making it illegal to be part of a "criminal organization" becomes much easier to pursue when street gangs self-identify as a criminal entity by adopting a name. Consistent with this observation, new-age gang players arrested pursuant to the multijurisdictional investigation described in Chap. 1 denied any affiliation to the "Born to Kill" gang, while simultaneously admitting to various levels of participation in the events outlined. In view of the mobility associated with new-age street gangs, and the ensuing arrests that revealed the gang players in that multi-jurisdictional investigation were from the United States—two from Los Angeles in particular—it is reasonable to suggest that they were also very aware of the existence of existing American legislation such as the State of California's *Street Terrorism, Enforcement and Protection Act 1991*; an Act that was designed to significantly lengthen the court sentences given to those convicted of gang activity.

The irony associated with gang names remains with the observation that they have—in the occidental gang paradigm that has long prevailed in North America—been traditionally associated with geographic "turf". And while the sharing of gang names by police investigators to the public-at-large is a way of building community capacity and raising community consciousness as it pertains to gang activity, the reality is, that the names adopted by gangs today are far more motivated by external imposition than an internal sense of group identity. While gang names are often given by rivals in the criminal subculture, they have also been the result of attributions made by police in attempts to gain analytical insight into a fluid gang structure that presents as a "mix-and-match" configuration of players and undermines police attempts to establish suspect descriptions that can be shared across jurisdictions.[4]

Leaving the Gang

In sharp contrast to the occidental gang model, the new-age gang's fluidity allows players to disassociate themselves from future gang activity at any time. The most frequent reason provided was aging and the desire to legitimize their activities. As was explained by a now 'retired' street gang leader, he continues to be the recipient of respect from the street gang players because of his background and previous connections. It is important to note however, that what he meant by respect was actually a reference to the reality that his business had never been the recipient of extortion attempts, frequently disguised as "protection money". "Protection" at its base is actually what business merchants need should they refuse extortion payments from a street gang leader's "boys", but because of this individual's past and lingering connections, no one had dared come to his place of business imposing their protective services.

The second reason offered for leaving gang life was for the purposes of marriage and starting a family. By assuming this new role, the individual was expected to demonstrate respect for his wife and her family; a perspective that lends insight into a dimension of culture that places an emphasis on the collective "face" as opposed to the individual's actions being a reflection only on himself. Changing responsibilities pursuant to marriage is not confined to gang participation alone, and has indeed been offered by others as a reason generally for young males to alter their lifestyle and redefine their personal network (Boswell 1969). In order to understand the significance of this insight, it is necessary to refer to the cultural differences which exist between what we generally refer to as collectivist cultures

---

[4] The State of New Jersey Commission of Investigation made this observation in 1993 during their hearings into criminal street gangs.

as opposed to the North American-based individualist cultural model; a dichotomy that will be explored in Chap. 5.

The third reason offered for breaking with a street gang leader, occurred when an individual felt they had cultivated their own ego-centered following of potential players and now had sufficient resources to splinter off and rival other street gang leaders. Violence is the inevitable consequence of this rivalry because, in order to secure affiliation with organized crime and make money, it is first necessary to create a void by discrediting or destabilizing one of the affiliated street gang leaders.

The fourth reason provided for leaving the gang lifestyle can best be described as the duality of being "taken out" or "taken down". For some gang players, the violence associated with eruptions in gang rivalry reaches a threshold where they decide that the money to be made is not worth dying for; for others, targeted police enforcement increases the chances of being "taken down" by criminal prosecution, hence they too decide to leave the lifestyle.

A lesser recognized explanation of why some players leave the gang lifestyle was provided by an organized crime-level informant. He related an instance wherein a street gang leader had engaged in freelance criminal activity by committing violent armed robberies to businesses dealing in high-end commodities. These robberies were occurring during the day in areas frequented by high volumes of pedestrian traffic and had garnered much unwanted attention from the police, media, and local politicians; a reckless undertaking that had the potential of bringing equally unwelcome attention to the activities of those at the organized crime level. As a result, this particular street gang leader was advised that he no longer "followed" the organized crime group and his affiliation was terminated. As a result of this imposed exile, the leader and his players were moved out of their money-making comfort zone and, as an ensuing consequence, the leader was forced to resort to higher risk and lower gain criminal activity less familiar to him and which led to his imminent arrest.

Whatever the motivation for leaving the gang lifestyle or shifting allegiances to a street gang leader, what is clear is that among new-age gangs exhibiting the dimensions of fluidity and mobility, they can leave the gang life at any time as long as they show loyalty to the money-making enterprise that persists, through their continued silence. As a street gang player explained to me, gang participation is "all about making money and using somebody to do it. When you make enough money, you leave". In part, this ability to leave the lifestyle is intricately connected to the observation that participation was but one of the ways in which the players were associated. Players are activated preferentially by street gang leaders through their personal network of relationships and associations, therefore although this one strand of the relationship is severed, other strands in what can be described as a multiplex relationship remain intact.

References

Boswell, D. M. (1969). Personal crises and the mobilization of the social network. In J. Clyde Mitchell (Ed.), *Social networks in urban situations*. Manchester: Manchester University Press.

Hagan, F. (1983). The organized crime continuum: a further specification of a new conceptual model. *Criminal Justice Review, 8*, 52–57.

Sessions, W. S. (1991). *Proceedings of the permanent subcommittee on investigations*. Washington: U.S. Government Printing Office.

State of New Jersey Commission of Investigation. (1993). *Criminal street gangs*. Trenton NJ: State of New Jersey.

Chapter 4
Criminal Enterprise

> *The most powerful gang is the most violent gang.*
> *With violence you get power, and with power you get money.*

In this chapter, I have chosen to reference the criminal activity associated with new-age gangs as "criminal enterprise"; a term which has long been applied to criminal endeavours that recognize the interplay between street gangs, their affiliation with organized crime, and their placement within the context of a criminal organizational structure. By pursuing an "enterprise" approach, it allows us to focus our attention on the revenue-generating efforts of a criminal organization, rather than on the individual players within that organizational structure; players who are already acknowledged to be fluid in their participation within a new-age gang.

New-age gangs are primarily engaged in criminal activity which can be characterized as high risk for medium to low-gain, contingent on whether they have affiliation with an organized crime group. For those gangs who have not yet secured affiliation, high-risk and low-gain criminal activities requiring comparatively little long-range planning and a *modus operandi* predicated on instilling fear in victims, such as armed robberies, home-invasion robberies, protection rackets, and extortion, remain their primary source of revenue. Drug distribution, weapons running, financial crimes, prostitution, and assigned protections to sites of illegal activity, are those that remain assigned to street gangs as a result of their affiliation with an organized crime group. Discussion in this chapter will focus on those activities that remain within the purview of freelance activities undertaken by new-age gangs to either supplement income, or which are commonly resorted to when disaffiliated with organized crime. It is not within the scope of this particular undertaking to examine each of the specific types of criminal activity reliant on the importation and distribution networks of organized crime. It is sufficient to say however, that the on-the-ground movement, distribution, and protection of commodities imported by organized crime—be they property or person—remain

---

An observation shared by a police gang investigator, based on what an organized crime level informant related to him.

reliant on a street gang leader and his following for their distribution or destination-delivery, and collection.

Extortion

A predictable source of gang income stems from the systematic extortion of legitimate businesses, particularly those of an ethnocultural background familiar to the street gang leader. As explained by a gang informant, there exists a tendency to extort your own because "if they are from the same background they know the unwritten rules, but when you deal outside your community you don't have the same powers to deal with them like you can your own." This same informant went on to elaborate on what specific "powers" the gangs had to deal with those unwilling to comply with extortion demands and why victims were reluctant to report the extortionists to police:

> Witnesses are telling me how relatives are getting threatening calls, threatening letters, visits from people back in their home country telling them not to testify. That's how far reaching it is. If you move outside your own community into another ethnic group, you don't have the same control.

According to police sources, extortions can be categorized as direct or indirect, and as either carrying a time-deadline or weekly instalments. The particular *modus operandi* selected by street gang extortionists will vary, however despite how subtle the message conveyed may be, its loosest translation always translates to "comply or suffer the consequences". To demonstrate the subtle difference between a direct and indirect method of extortion, the following conversation shared with police, represents a typical indirect form of extortion which occurred to a restaurant owner:

> Caller: I have a bunch of kids. They have no place to live. I want you to help them out. I'm sure you know what I mean.
> (Victim states that she does not understand what he means.)
> Caller: Well, I've been calling many times. I've been patient enough. I don't want the kids to come down. I'm just talking for them. You are in business. You don't want someone to come and ruin the business by turning over a few tables or use something to point at you.
> (Victim states to caller that the police frequent her business.)
> Caller: The police can't protect you all the time. You can get $500 or $600 dollars. I know you have people watching your place to protect your place. I saw you pay other people.

Generally speaking collectivist and high-context cultures favor an indirect form of extortion whereby threats are implied, as opposed to using the more direct approach favored by low-context cultures.[1] The ethnic of non-confrontation that is manifest among collectivist cultures supports the indirect form of extortion which preserves the public "face" of the individual being extorted. This will be further developed in Chap. 5 as it pertains to "culture in the shadows". Frequently during extortions in connection with business establishments, the extortionist will offer protection in return for the money being extorted, as opposed to an outright demand for money. Often when protection is offered and the victim refuses the services, the establishment is damaged in order to demonstrate the need for the victim to acquire protection and thereby accede to the extortion demands. The damage to the premises would then be followed up by a return visit to the merchant by street gang players and the suggestion made that they be hired to protect the premises from further risk of damage.

The gimmicks used during extortion attempts are as varied as those using them, and range from outright intimidation and threats to the victim's well being, to subtle and implied requests for financial assistance based on alleged humanitarian reasons. What is acknowledged is that the use of extortions as a source of street gang income is more widespread than the number of offences reported to police would indicate. A former street gang leader—turned business operator—revealed that among other owners he spoke with, "Seventy percent of the time businessmen talk business, but thirty percent of the time they talk about extortion." Protection money achieved through extortion remains a predictable source of street gang income, primarily because of its outward invisibility and a fear among those being extorted to report it to police. The reluctance among merchants and residents to report victimization to police has been attributed to a combination of both the fear of gang retaliation that might lead to more severe repercussions, and as one informant explained:

> If you have an active element within a community purporting that you can't trust the police because they treat ethnocultural groups differently, this type of thing causes community members to be even more reluctant to report victimization.

Protection Rackets

In contrast to merchant extortions, gang revenues generated by providing assigned "protection" to gaming dens or bawdy houses operated by the organized crime group a gang leader follows, tends to be a more predictable source of income. But, as the following quote by a police investigator tasked with dismantling illegal gaming operations illustrates, it can also be more susceptible to police interruption:

---

[1] The terms "low-context" and "high-context" were first used by the anthropologist Edward T. Hall to dichotomize between cultures that utilize direct (low-context) or indirect (high-context) styles of communication.

He (organized crime level figure) actually said that if we didn't lay off the gambling houses, we as police cause violent crime because he can't control his 'boys'; they have bills. He says they can't do it without gambling money, so they turn to extortion and that if we let him run his games uninterrupted, in return he would give us anyone we were looking for.

Through attachment to the organized crime group, the street gang leader will secure additional employment in the gambling dens, bawdy houses, and protection rackets operated by the organization; their role being to ensure that only regular or known clientele frequent the establishment, provide an armed presence within the premises, and conduct follow-up debt collection should it be required.

Protection rackets and extortions represent two halves of the same whole that recognizes protection as both a precursor to, and a consequence of, extortions. Because of this duality, hiring the protection of street gangs is no assurance of security, either to the person or property. When intergang hostilities arise, street gangs frequently engineer robberies on each other's "protected" clients in order to undermine the credibility of the gang furnishing the protection, or alternatively, will alert police to a location of protected illegal activity so that the police dismantle the illegal operation. In either scenario, the street gang leader's following providing the protection at these locations are discredited in their inability to ensure a safe environment for the unlawful activity, and patrons are left with the notion that an establishment is unsafe. The "guns for hire" status that characterizes twenty first century street gangs is such that the more ruthless and violent a street gang leader is, the more successful they will be in securing affiliation with an organized crime group.

Home Invasions

A trademark of street gang activity has been the armed robbery of private homes, also known as the home invasion robbery. Dubbed the "crime of the 1990′s" by police and media headlines, it remains one of the most effective means by which street gangs ensure compliance. Street gangs use the home invasion robbery as a means of extorting money from targets by terrorizing their families. Frequently individuals are targeted because the gangs become aware that large amounts of cash and jewellery are kept in the home; an occurrence that is particularly an issue among those with limited English language skills who may mistrust the banking system. While money is generally the motive behind home invasion robberies, revenge is also a reason for the victim intimidation, humiliation, and violence that accompanies this type of offence. Police sources have revealed that street gang players frequently travel to other jurisdictions to extort and commit home invasion robberies, as assistance to local players who are too well known. When home invasion robberies occur in the absence of any substantial amount of cash or jewellery in the home, it can be reasonably suggested that they are motivated by revenge as opposed to misinformation "slip-ups" by gang leaders, who are noted for the degree of effort expended in compiling information on the habits and daily activities of intended victims. If revenge is the motive behind a home invasion robbery, then it is likely that it is either punishment for a lack of co-operation during past extortion attempts or it is intended to instil sufficient fear in a victim so as to secure future compliance.

The success of home invasion robberies depends on the victim's fear of retaliation by gang members and a sense of vulnerability should the offender be apprehended, charged, and released back to the street pending trial. It is this fear of retaliation that keeps instances of both protection extortions and home invasions predictable methods of ensuring a street gang leader's payroll.

For a street gang leader, the appeal of "following" an established organized crime leader remains, in part, with the protection jobs the street gang leader is hired for and the extortion money that can be extracted from merchants because of the street gang leader's affiliation and reputation for violence. An added incentive among street gang leaders for following an organized crime level leader is the opportunity that exists to be pulled up the structural ladder because of the success shown in generating money at the street gang level.

Armed Robbery

Armed robbery is a lucrative pastime of street gangs, with jewellery stores, gambling dens, restaurants, and more recently electronics wholesalers, presenting as targets of choice among street gangs.

In an attempt to lend perspective to the amount of gang revenue generated by a "typical" jewellery store robbery, a netting of $100,000 in jewellery would generally result in a return of approximately 10–20 % or between $10,000 and $20,000 payment to the street gang leader in order that he, in turn, could compensate his core group and action-set associates.[2] The remainder goes up the organized crime level through an organized crime level conduit responsible for the liquidation of stolen jewellery. While the street gang leader hands the jewellery over to the contact through which he is directed to deal, the money that the street gang leader receives as payment is predetermined by higher levels within the organized crime structure. If street gang leaders want greater payment, then they are on their own to freelance and will need to cultivate their own buyers who are willing to take the risk and give out a greater percentage of payment. While freelancing by street gang leaders in the pursuit of money is tolerated, too much unwanted attention as a result of this activity carries with it the risk of becoming a liability to the business pursuits of the organized crime group. In the event of this scenario occurring, out of town street gang leaders who are not known to police are frequently activated, and in return, locally affiliated street gang leaders will be loaned out for reciprocal out-of-town jobs.

---

[2] The amounts cited were shared by a street gang leader during interviews with this author.

Intergang Rivalry

While armed robberies are generally for the purposes of meeting financial commitments, unaffiliated street gangs will preferentially target premises that are receiving the protective services of another street gang; the intent being to discredit the street gang providing the protection, and to convey to the level of organized crime that the affiliated gang is incapable of providing adequate protection. During these robberies it is not uncommon for patrons inside the targeted premises to be robbed of personal property including identification, leaving them both unlikely to return to the establishment, but also reluctant to cooperate with police investigators knowing that those responsible for the robbery now know who they are and where they live. Robberies of this nature that include the patrons inside as targets, can be considered message robberies and should be viewed as a preincident indicator of simmering intergang rivalries between a gang leader and his following that are affiliated with organized crime and making money, and those unaffiliated but vying for work from that same level. An awareness of this ever-present threat among street gangs is reflected in the following quote from a police investigator tasked with making a forced entry into an illegal bawdy house. He describes the preferred interpretation for those inside the premises when inter-gang rivalries have erupted:

> When they (those inside the premises) hear the bang, they'll know it's one of two things (rival gang or police) and they'll be glad it's us (the police).

Although intergang hostilities occur at the street gang level, they are generally engineered among rival gang leaders positioning for affiliation at the level of organized crime. Emerging street gang leaders will constantly try to establish themselves as more ruthless than the following of existing street gang leaders; a tactic that is used to attract the attention of those who have hired the street gang leader currently providing protection to the money-generating venue. And, while I have chosen to reference this type of gang rivalry as intergang rivalry, it is important to emphasize that is has been used to dichotomize against intragang rivalries; a term that is, in itself, inherently contradictory as it is better conceived of as occurring within a street gang leader's ego-centred network. As described in the Chap. 2 discussion of networks, each member of a leader's ego-centred network is themselves the centre of a plurality of relations, with the ability to activate their own coalition of followers; their success in being able to do so however, is contingent on their ability to maintain a payroll commitment. Once this ability is acquired, a leader will be spawned and the potential for rivalry between the existing and newly emerging leaders, and their respective followings, exists. Intergang rivalries as manifested through an escalation in violence among players remains a key insight into the existence of a power struggle at the level of new-age street gang leaders.

Chapter 5
Culture in the Shadows

> *Culture is the "lens" through which we view the world; the "logic" by which we order it; the "grammar" by which it makes sense.*

The examples included for discussion in this chapter include both insights and rationales provided by informants, which came to the fore during the interview process and suggested a cultural basis, either expressly stated or implied.

Before embarking on a discussion of how culture might have influenced the actions and decisions pursued by new-age gang leaders and "players" in the examples that follow, it is first useful to include a definition of culture. Because situational analysis was utilized as a research methodology for its utility in providing a framework of analysis for the 'on-the-ground' decisions made by new-age gang leaders, I have chosen to adopt the following definition of culture from cognitive anthropology; a definition which is consistent with the use of situational analysis:

> Culture [then] is not only observable behavior but the shared ideals, values, and beliefs people use to interpret experience and generate behavior and that are reflected by their behavior (Haviland et al. 2009, p. 34).

Patterns of Victimization

In response to interview questions that probed the selection of victims and business premises that were targeted for monetary gain, the leader of a Vietnamese street gang once explained that he considered himself to be "100 % Vietnamese"; a self-identification that rested with the place of birth of grandparents. This particular street gang leader proceeded to draw a clear distinction between his ethnocultural identity and that of others he selected for victimization. While this particular leader's self-identification as ethnic-Vietnamese served to justify the selection of

---

This quote is attributed to anthropologists Kevin Avruch and Peter Black (1993).

C. E. Prowse, *Defining Street Gangs in the 21st Century*, SpringerBriefs in Criminology, DOI: 10.1007/978-1-4614-4307-0_5, © The Author(s) 2012

other individuals and merchants—in particular ethnic-Chinese Vietnamese—as targets of choice, he also used it to eliminate his "own people" from the same fate. The manifestation of ethnocultural self-identification extending back three generations being applied to the selection of victim targets, is an important revelation and one in which it is reasonable to suggest may extend to other attributions likewise being applied to patterns of victimization. In this particular example, the external application of *emic*[1] criteria to others was justified by long-standing hostilities and political cleavages in the country of birth of grandparents.

While ethnocultural self-identification was used to justify excluding potential victims, however it was equally observed to be used in the selection of business operators for the purposes of extortion and protection. As explained by a community-of-interest business leader who commented on the prevalence of protection payments among those with whom he regularly liaised:

> They stick to their own because they are aware everybody has come from the same background. With their own group, everybody knows the rules … the unwritten rules, but when you deal with outside your community, you don't have the same powers to deal with them like you can with your own.

An organized crime level informant also alluded to ethnocultural alignment at the level of street gang leaders, and suggested that those who were of a mixed ethnocultural background were actually of more use to him for "business" purposes by virtue of their multilingual fluency.

While the application of ethnocultural criteria to victim selection remained variable between street gang leaders, it nonetheless remained a criterion. It was offered by informants to justify both victim selection and exclusion, and, in the example provided by the organized crime conduit, was offered as a preferred characteristic for street gang leaders seeking affiliation with organized crime.

The type of ethnocultural distinction previously described was also seen to manifest in rivalries between street gang players who were observed to frequently resort to the imposition of *emic* descriptors to gang players following a different street gang leader. Names attributed to rivals such as "Fresh off the Boat" and the "FK's"—short for "Fresh off the Boat Killers"—are examples that originated in this author's policing jurisdiction and that reflect the imposition of an attribution to justify hostilities that extend beyond economic rivalries.[2] In this particular example, the length of time since immigration from offshores by parents was the target of the imposed attribution. While the affiliation within these two street gangs did reflect some ethnocultural alignment among the players activated through the street gang leader from his network of associations, it was by no means absolute.

---

[1] An *emic* terminology or perspective is one that is shared by insiders to the phenomenon under discussion; in this instance among gang leaders and players.

[2] The two gangs mentioned were engaged in a protracted period of intergang warfare in Calgary, Alberta, Canada that spanned the years 2003–2009. The explanation for the attribution of gang names was provided to this author by a community-of-interest informant.

An externally imposed ethnocultural affiliation did however, delineate a social–structural boundary between gang players following different leaders; some leaders affiliated at the level of organized crime and some not.

Concept of "Gang"

Traditionally among North American gangs modeled in the occidental paradigm of geographic control and fixed anchorage, the definition of a "gang" was somewhat consistent across police jurisdictions. The street gangs were modeled after an individualist cultural paradigm that favored them as a distinct group that remained together as a circumscribed entity, and possessed a group identity distinct from other spheres of associations and relationships. By contrast, new-age gangs are but one instance of relationships that are drawn from a much wider network of associations based on many factors: kinship, friendships, and economic contacts. The control of geographic "turf" for the purposes of making money is replaced by economic and commodity-based "turf", whereby the gang players follow their distribution networks regardless of geography. It is this characteristic of mobility across jurisdictional boundaries that frequently results in encroachment into the 'turf' of geographically anchored gangs and most readily escalates into 'turf' wars.

If an individualist versus collectivist typology[3] were to be applied to the two models of gang structure as noted—occidental and new-age, respectively—the differences are somewhat accounted for. The individualist model captures the structure long-associated with occidental street gangs if we consider the occidental gang as a basis of self-identity as a gang member. By conceiving of it in this way, we see occidental gangs as representing a set-apart entity wherein power differentials exist within prescribed individual roles which are clearly defined; rites of passage delimit participation; behavioral codes enforce compliance and loyalty; and the members assume a gang identity. Although they engage in criminal activity as members of the gang, their positioning within that collective is analogous to "mainstream" individualist participation in community associations.

By contrast, if we similarly apply a collectivist orientation to "new-age" gangs, we see that the players mobilized through the street gang leader are already drawn from a personal network of relations who represent a coalition of varying durations; loyalty is vested in the task at hand; in-group compliance is ensured through the communication style favored by the gang leader, as opposed to power differentials inherent in prescribed roles within occidental gangs; and once the task

---

[3] Hofstede et al. (2010) explain "individualism" (high IDV score) as the extent to which people choose to live with an emphasis on personal identity, while "collectivism" (low IDV score) refers to an emphasis on a group identity. The majority of the world's cultures are individualist in nature and exhibit a high IDV score. In collectivist cultures (low IDV), members tend to work as a group oftentimes to the point of suppressing their own ideas or suggestions in order to ensure in-group cooperation. Individual gains are subordinated to those that benefit the group as a whole.

at hand is complete, the coalition ceases to exist and the participants resume their place in the street gang leader's diverse social network.

Concept of "Face" or Respect

The notion of "face" among those following a collectivist cultural paradigm is an intricate concept that shows two distinct aspects: "having face" and "giving face". "Having face" represents the ability to demonstrate power and influence without resorting to overt intimidation tactics, but in order to wield this level of influence the individual concerned must have already demonstrated the ability to deliver on past threats of violence or harm, implied or otherwise.

"Giving face" involves the paying of respect, deference, or gang "gentleman-liness", as a way of placating someone who has been offended or presents an impediment to future business. Generally, this type of "face" is directed toward those who are on the receiving end of a potential embarrassment and associated "loss of face" situation or toward those to which some form of compensation is owed, such as a victim or witness destined for court. Giving "face" is also frequently demonstrated in extortion attempts that avoid the use of overt threats such as "or else" and opt for softer approaches such as inferences which favor a less threatening terminology and, in so doing, preserve the victim's "face" or self-esteem. This approach is intricately tied to the ethic of non-confrontation that characterizes high-context cultural orientations and, as a behavioral ethic it ensures the public "face" of individuals is respected in the eyes of others.[4] Exercising the ethic of non-confrontation finds expression in active encounters where the element of choice does not exist and where the effects of power differentials—real or perceived—manifest as the extorter with the power dictating, and the recipient exhibiting compliance. Simply stated, "face" is the respect shown to someone out of respect for their position of power or for their potential to negatively impact your life. In the criminal world, "face" provided in the form of a monetary bribe or "tribute" remains a significant reason why victims and witnesses often choose to recant statements made to police or choose not to cooperate with the criminal justice system. The following observation was shared by a police gang investigator who felt he was being stonewalled in securing witness and victim compliance:

> My witnesses are telling me how relatives back home [source country] are getting threatening calls, threatening letters, visits from people telling them not to testify. That's how far reaching it is. If you move outside your own community into another ethnic group, you don't have the same control.

---

[4] Hall (1976) developed use of the terms "low-context" and "high-context" to dichotomize different cultural emphases placed on the context surrounding one's actions. Hofstede (1983) applied a similar dichotomy to cultures worldwide using the terms "individualist" and "collectivist" according to the primacy placed on the individual or the group collective.

	Low-Context	High-Context
	Individual focused	Group focused
	Focus on the verbal	Focus on the setting
	Emphasis on the message	Emphasis on relationship
	Emphasis on *what* is said	Emphasis on *how* it is said
	Heterogeneous beliefs	Homogeneous beliefs

Fig. 5.1 Low/high context cultures continuum (This chart has been adapted from Hall's (1976) discussion of a high-context and low-context cultures continuum.)

What is important to emphasize at this juncture, is that the majority of the world is modeled after a high-context and collectivist cultural identity (Hofstede et al. 2010) that emphasizes group-focused achievement, which in-turn is preserved through adherence to cultural ethics and rules of behavior that include the ethic of non-confrontation. Employing the "giving of face" to gang members as a means to overcome their feelings of having been "disrespected"—by other gang members or the community—is a strategy that has received increased attention. It is currently being used by law enforcement in Chicago as part of the community project "Ceasefire" in an effort to stop the violence between rival gangs.[5] While inherent limitations for terminating gang rivalries predicated on controlling money-making turf are fully recognized, the attempts to date do carry the promise of diminishing life-threatening violence in highly frequented public venues. Figure 5.1 depicts salient cultural differences along a high-context/low-context cultures continuum.

Public Space

The notion of public space is a variable that differs cross-culturally and carries with it the promise of lending insight into how street gangs view their activities. New-age gang players exhibiting the dimensions of fluidity of gang participation and mobility across a geographic landscape, tend to be more consistent with a collectivist cultural paradigm that views public space as outside the control of a particular group. By contrast, street gangs modeled in the long-standing occidental paradigm of geographic anchorage, would appear to view public space as

---

[5] In four of seven Chicago sites, the introduction of CeaseFire-Chicago was found to be associated with "distinct and statistically significant" declines in actual and attempted shootings. These declines ranged from 17–24 % in contrast to other matched comparison areas (Skogan et al. 2008, p. 3).

something within their control and which must be defended against encroachment. Suffice it to say that with these conflicting notions, there exists an everpresent potential for escalating tensions and violent confrontation as these divergent perceptions of public space—presenting as geographic "turf"—come into contract with one another.

Support for my belief that culture exists "in the shadows" and should be considered in instances where there occur seemingly difficult to account for elements of gang activity, was reinforced over time through the protracted interview process. The use of the word "obligation" to assist family was a theme that regularly emerged and the choice of the word proved to be very deliberate. During one of my interviews with a street gang player with whom I spoke frequently—both inside and outside of prison—he corrected my reference to his attempts to financially assist his family as an "expectation". In his particular circumstance as a first generation Canadian, I came to view him as an individual inextricably embedded in a complex social network of specific "obligations" associated with unconditional financial assistance to family. Unable to meet these financial obligations through legitimate means, new-age gang participation provided a means of acquiring ready access to cash. The pressures created by the conflicting demands of a culturally rooted financial obligation to assist family, and the lack of a legitimate means of fulfilling that obligation, were never expressed more cogently than they were by him. Reflecting on his intermittent, yet long-standing involvement with a new-age gang, and the lengthy prison sentence he had now served, he explained that for him gang involvement was not a "mistake" because the word mistake implies choice. In his words, "It was not a mistake. I had no choice."

References

Avruch, K., & Black, P. (1993). Conflict resolution and intercultural settings: Problems and prospects. In D. Sandale & H. Van der Merwe (Eds.), *Conflict resolution theory and practice: Integration and application*. New York: St. Martin's Press.

Hall, E. T. (1976). *Beyond culture*. New York: Doubleday.

Haviland, W. A., Fedorak, S. A., & Lee, R. B. (2009). *Cultural anthropology* (3rd Canadian ed.). Toronto: Nelson.

Hofstede, G. (1983). Culture's consequences: International differences in work-related values. *Administrative Science Quarterly, 28*(4), 625–629.

Hofstede, G., Hofstede, G. S., & Minkow, M. (2010). *Cultures and organizations: Software of the mind* (3rd ed.). New York: McGraw Hill.

Skogan, W. G., Hartnett, S. M., Bump, N., & Dubois, J. (2008). *Evaluation of CeaseFire-Chicago*. Chicago: Northwestern University.

Chapter 6
Frequently Asked Questions

The following section has been included in an attempt to respond to those questions that have been most frequently asked of this author both by the media and the community-at-large, during interviews that now number in the hundreds. Although not exhaustive, the questions selected for inclusion do represent those whose answers will reinforce key elements discussed in this text, if the "new-age" gang problem is to be managed. Readers will note that the word "managed" is being specifically selected, so as to give recognition to the structural dimension of street gangs; their interface with organized crime, and; their potential for transnational connections and mobility. To suggest that the street gang phenomena can be eliminated is to have failed to recognize what this text has endeavored to explain: New-age street gangs are born of, and remain, intricately intertwined with leader-centred relationship-based social networks of interaction.

The answers to the questions that follow are presented in a stand-alone manner and do not necessarily presume that those reading this section have read the text in its entirety. For that reason, the style favored here could be characterized as direct, and, with the exception of necessary attribution, devoid of research references previously included in the corpus of the text.

Unless otherwise stated, the questions that follow are being addressed from a paradigm of new-age gangs; the title of this book.

Why does Violence Spontaneously Erupt?

Violence is a reality of street gang existence which, at its simplest, is all about making money. Street gangs will always rival for affiliation at the level of organized crime, so intergang rivalry is the inevitable consequence of that. What is most frequently occurring when violence erupts is that one group is affiliated at the level of organized crime and making money, and another or others are similarly structured and are now in a position to rival the group that is affiliated. Factions within an affiliated street gang leader's own group also possess the ability to form their own

C. E. Prowse, *Defining Street Gangs in the 21st Century*, SpringerBriefs in Criminology,   43
DOI: 10.1007/978-1-4614-4307-0_6, © The Author(s) 2012

leader-centred network, break off, structure, and in turn similarly rival. The length of calms in between escalating tensions and spates of violence is somewhat connected to where in the gang organizational structure those who may have been killed or arrested were; how reliant was the street gang leader on the activation of this player. A loss of expertise in the street gang leader's following will lead to a longer period of destabilization, until the time when the street gang leader identifies someone to fill the void created. Death and jail remain two ways in which gangs are destabilized, either due to a loss of expertise or a loss of leadership. The longer the calm between spates of violence, the more likely it is that the person arrested or killed was a more frequent and preferentially activated "player" by the street gang leader.

Why do the Gangs Seem to be Along Ethnic Lines?

If a street gang leader is of a particular ethnocultural background, then you indeed may see some ethnocultural alignment, but only to the extent that it is generally recognized that those you trust—particularly for this type of high-risk criminal activity—are generally drawn from those with whom you live, work, or play. The perception of ethnocultural alignment is an artifact that is by no means an absolute, and it is indeed risky for investigative pursuits to proceed along that premise. In reality, you can be "polka-dotted" or striped in appearance but, if you can further the money-making agenda of a new-age street gang leader, you are in.

Another facet of the perception of ethnocultural alignment among street gangs is the dimension of networks. If your importation networks are sourced in a particular area of the world, as is the particular case with drug importations, then there may very likely be ethnocultural alignment from that area in order to facilitate on-the-ground distribution of that commodity. In short, those you know and trust are generally drawn from those whom you already know, or have come to know, through current and past live, work, or play sites.

Why are Witnesses and Informants Hard to Find?

The "code of silence" that police have referred to when stifled in their investigative quests for community members to come forward with information concerning gang activities, has different dimensions that need to be emphasized.

First, the fear of gang tentacles reaching back to family members locally or elsewhere—whether real or perceived—is a fear that is very real in the mind of the person being threatened. A predictable source of revenue for street gang leaders—affiliated with organized crime and unaffiliated gangs alike—comes from gang extortion and protection rackets. Both remain extremely lucrative and are based on the fear generated on the part of the victim merchants and businesses that have experienced threats or home invasions as a way of securing their compliance in the paying of "protection".

The second dimension to this question pertains to the cultural ethic of "face", expressed alternatively as the deference shown to someone out of respect for their position of power or for their position in your life. In the criminal world, it can be a powerful motivation for victims and witnesses to make the choice to either recant their original version of events as related to police, or they may refuse to cooperate or come forward with information in the first instance. Gang members will frequently attempt to reach out with monetary "tributes" to those who have been victimized or present as potential witnesses, as a way of dissuading them from coming forward and, just as often as this may occur, it carries with it the potential to achieve the desired result. The cultural ethic of "face" cannot be overstated and indeed, remains a primary reason why gang players themselves choose to leave the lifestyle, frequently due to changing family roles and responsibilities. If they have made enough money to assist or support family, managed to not get caught by police or 'taken out' by rivals, they will leave the lifestyle to safeguard their family physically and, in some instances, to fulfill a cultural expectation that places an emphasis on not bringing disgrace to the family name. The cultural ethos described as "face" or respect flows from what we term a "collectivist" cultural orientation which emphasizes a group focus and the importance of "face" or family reputation.

A third dimension to the existence of a "code of silence" surrounding community cooperation has to do with its negative impact on investigative timeliness. Witnesses who come forward early into police investigations carry with them the potential to further police investigative evidence collection. This, in turn, can serve to reduce the emphasis that will be placed on court witnesses by supplementing, or even replacing, witness testimony with physical evidence. For community members to not come forward with what they have seen or heard, assists only the gangs, however this should in no way trivialize the fear a witness experiences, as real.

Do Community-Based Programs Work?

One dimension of community-based initiatives that is vital to police gang investigative efforts is the need for police officers to be a frequent presence at community events, and at businesses in the areas frequented by suspected gang players or leaders as known life, work, or play sites. If the police are an everpresent fixture in these areas, then it becomes easier for those with information to share it with the police without being detected as the source of that information. If police are in constant contact with a community of interest and are seen to be regularly stopping by and interacting with areas they suspect are frequented by gang players, then conversations between the police and the community become a nonevent; potentially to the point that the gangs will not know when the information was passed or by whom. They may have general suspicions, but general suspicions become hard to punish or respond to without the potential for a great deal of unwanted public, police, and media attention. The last thing a street gang leader wants is to attract a lot of unwanted attention to his activities; that is bad for his individual criminal pursuits and particularly unwanted at the level of the organized crime group with which he may be affiliated and relying on to meet his payroll.

Is Solving the Gang Problem an Issue of Increased Police Numbers?

Injecting more police officers into gang investigation and suppression always helps, but determining how and where manpower should be deployed is what will ultimately dictate how quickly a threshold of effectiveness is achieved. More police officers will always assist gang investigations, if only to the extent that it will reduce deployment concerns and allow police to 'switch gears' quickly to respond to changing intelligence information and the shifting priorities that flow from that information. Effective police intelligence efforts carry with it the potential to focus investigative efforts at a higher level in the criminal organizational structure than just that of street gang players. When this happens, you can bring unwanted attention to bear on the level of organized crime which can, in turn, cause street gang leaders who may have been involved in more sensationalized events that have presented a risk to public safety, to be cut adrift from their organized crime-level affiliation. The last thing organized crime groups want is attention brought to their activities by a rogue street gang leader. When a street gang leader is cut adrift, he too has a payroll to meet and is forced out of his comfort zone and into higher risk freelance activities that present a greater potential for being apprehended. Frequently, the types of freelance activities that ensue are armed robberies of high-end jewellery stores or other commodity business operations that are generally located in very public domains and carry with them an increased number of potential witnesses.

How are the Gangs Structured?

This text has chosen to use the term "new-age" to reflect how street gangs have been structuring over the past 15+ years, depending on the North American jurisdiction. The long-standing North American model of gangs—frequently referred to as occidental gangs—is the one that has been the prevailing North American model for gang criminal activity dating back to the 1960s and, as some would argue, even earlier. These gangs are geographically anchored in their activities in that they control a very circumscribed area of a city or geographic area that is recognized as their 'turf' and generally visible to all who pass through. They are very demonstrative in laying ownership to a geographic turf because control over that area is their criminal livelihood. They control the criminal activity and money flowing from that activity within that area and, if they do not maintain control, they run the risk of losing their money-making ability. It is therefore very much in their best interests to be noticed and seen to be in control; acts of intimidation are very overt and fuel this necessity. Consistent with this paradigm, the membership is fixed, frequently engages in initiations or beating-in, and, as a member, you are initiated for life. But these no longer are representative of the gangs making the big money; they remain street gangs, but with only a very limited distribution network. By contrast, new-age gangs are fluid in their membership and mobile across geographic jurisdictions. The fluidity of their membership is why I have preferred to call them "players", because they exhibit an "in and out", "mix and match", "mobilized or not" style of participation, and all at the direction of a street gang leader. The street gang leader remains the key individual in the life of new-age gangs; the players are all known to him and it is he who decides whom to activate for specific types of criminal activity. The new-age gangs are not associated with geographic "turf", but rather, engage in commodity-based or economic "turf". Not unlike their occidental gang counterparts, they too deal in drugs—heroin, cocaine, ecstasy, marihuana—and additionally engage in 'muling' weapons, human trafficking, and other types of lucrative criminal activity that reflect their affiliation to organized crime. This affiliation allows them to share in the 'trickle down' distribution of commodities flowing from transnational and indeed transcontinental importation and distribution networks, hence they can be considered to control commodity-based turf as opposed to geographic turf. Gangs modeled in the paradigm of commodity-based distribution are, by necessity, mobile in their distribution pursuits; a characteristic that frequently results in encroachment into the money-making turf of those modeled in the paradigm of geographic anchorage and control. The two types of gangs can coexist, and indeed two or greater new-age gangs dealing in different commodities can overlap in their distribution networks, but this coexistence is tenuous at best and it is generally only a matter of time before encroachment on another gangs economic turf results and this is when the spates of violence erupt. It is this dimension of mobility across jurisdictions that bring new-age gangs most readily into conflict with other gangs that are geographically anchored. When tensions escalate and shootings erupt, they generally are levied at peripheral associates who are less involved and not expecting to be targeted. When this type of message shooting is sent and the group who has encroached chooses to continue, the violence is delivered more directly at actual members or players. Depending on the casualties taken-out by the shootings or those taken-down by subsequent police investigation into these acts, the violence may or may not quieten down. What is known, is that the length of calms in between these spates of violence is somewhat connected to how important the casualty was to the gang organizational structure; a structure that transcends individual players, however, expertise and/or leadership can take time to replace. What has been observed pursuant to police arrests is that the information supplied to them that has furthered their investigative efforts, has come from rival groups who have structured to the point that they are now rivalling the gang that is affiliated at the level of organized crime and making money. Highly publicized police take-downs, drug intercepts, and weapons transport intercepts, are prime examples of the types of tactics associated with rivals who have come to know the movements of other street gangs; knowledge they have acquired through the shifting allegiances that occurs among new-age street gangs players, particularly if a street gang leader is perceived to be in a position of vulnerability. Loyalty among street gang players is only to the money to be made; if that agenda is perceived to be in jeopardy, players will try to catch-on with another leader who is similarly mobilizing a following and preparing to rival for organized crime affiliation and a predictable source of revenue.

How do you Stop the Gangs From Recruiting Youth?

When we speak of street gangs recruiting young people into their ranks, it is important to address a couple of issues that influence this observation. If the street gang is modeled in the long-standing North American model of geographic anchorage and fixed membership, then the likelihood of reducing youth-at-risk indicators—such as exposure to known gang members and associates—will have an effect on stemming the flow of potential recruits through community-based efforts. Where these programs are particularly effective is actually one rung down in the "typology of groups" ladder at the level of "wannabe" groups. These are youth who are at the impressionable ages of 12–15 and who engage in impulsive and collective types of violence and intimidation toward other groups of youth. They want to be noticed, hence their name of "wannabe" or "want to be seen" as a gang member. They are very much in the public eye for their "notice me" types of antics, however, their criminal behavior is neither planned nor profitable and it is this dimension of making money on a predictable basis that sets them apart from the street gang. Anti-gang strategies are most effective if applied at this level because the attention they receive as a result of community intervention is the recognition they crave through their actions. They want to be seen as being of a concern and, if not addressed, they will become even a greater concern should they continue on in their criminal activity.

Community-based efforts have worked in many jurisdictions when applied to geographically anchored gangs and, because these gangs are geographically situated, community-based programs that focus on building community capacity within the areas where these gangs are operating, have also proven to effectively assist police investigative efforts where they have been used. New-age gangs modeled in a paradigm of fluidity of player participation and mobility across police jurisdictions have proven more difficult to impact. The dimensions of fluidity and mobility as instruments of organization have challenged community-based efforts and do emphasize the need for intelligence-based policing within a paradigm of community-based policing, toward identification of the street gang leader's social network of associates.

Is the Public More at Risk than Before?

With full recognition of the money to be made as a result of transnational importation and distribution commodity networks, the structuring of gangs will continue as will the rivalries between these groups as they vie for greater shares of the proverbial money pie. In the world of criminal organizations—of which gangs are the most visible dimension because of the high-risk, medium-gain types of activities they engage in—violence is a street gang leader's way of maintaining power and affiliation to the level of organized crime. With violence comes power, and with power comes the money to be made. If a street gang leader allows their self to be rivalled without answering those who challenge, the likelihood is that he would not be in power very long, at which time his money-making ability will be compromised and his following will leave. Loyalty in the world of new-age street gangs is only to the money to be made; when the money is gone, so are your players. It is this exact dimension that makes the street gang leader the key figure in the structure of new-age gangs: players who will be activated are of his choosing, they are mobilized through him, and the communication with them is from him directly. Those he chooses not to activate are left out of the communication loop; a flow of information they have no knowledge of and hence are of limited use to police as informants, should they choose to cooperate. What they can offer is limited to those activities they have participated in; an incentive to keep quiet about past activities and a reason why they can disassociate from further activity.

To address the issue of public risk, it is reasonable to suggest that those involved in street gangs know if and when they have crossed the proverbial "line" in their dealings with other groups or even within their own former group. We know factions splinter off regularly, structure, and try to rival a street gang leader that is affiliated at the level of organized crime and making money. When this happens, the player or players involved know they may be targeted, and they also know that the last thing gangs want to do is to risk killing an innocent bystander; a consequence that carries with it unwanted police, public, and media attention. For the gang player or leader who may be targeted, the safest place for them based on this realization is to travel and frequent very public places during peak activity times; locations that present a large number of potential witnesses that may pose a deterrent to those pursuing them. In other words, seek refuge in a public safety net. The corollary to this rationale, however is that if the only opportunity to target an otherwise hard to isolate gang player is in a public place, rivals will capitalize on that opportunity regardless of the public risk in doing so. If the high–risk shot is the only opportunity that presents itself for a target that is otherwise well insulated, and the stakes are high, then rivals will seize the opportunity regardless. This risk remains somewhat of an inevitability when intergang rivalry in particular escalates and has been witnessed in heavily travelled urban settings with increased frequency. What these plain view shootings should alert police to—particularly when they occur within a tight time frame—is that the gang rivals themselves perceive that there is an urgent need to resolve the power struggle between them. Inter—gang violence that escalates to lethal levels suggests that the gangs themselves have interpreted an urgent need to establish dominance; in all likelihood due to imminent money to be made and with little time remaining to demonstrate power and control.

Should Police Acknowledge a Gang's Existence?

A conventional wisdom today is that by denying the existence of gangs and the investigative challenges they have posed in the past, will ultimately only delay community mobilization and policing efforts. Having said that, police agencies in Canada and the United States that have had a long-standing proactive approach to crime have, by overwhelming majority, embarked on one of two strategies when confronted with gang phenomena.

The first strategy held to the doctrine that to acknowledge the existence of emerging gangs would only serve to give them the recognition they so desperately crave and, in so doing, perhaps fuel or accelerate their development.

The second strategy advocated that, at the very least, police should acknowledge their presence, if only to the extent that there are indications groups are in fact structuring or transitioning to planned and profitable activity—a hallmark of street gangs. A problem with the former option in my opinion is that by not going to the community with your information, you run the risk of silencing and marginalizing the many eyes and ears of a public who may be willing to provide information before these groups become too entrenched and too intimidating. By not accelerating your interaction with the community to meet an emerging presence—"wannabe" or otherwise—you are only postponing an inevitability, and, by so doing, placing yourself in a potential position of "catch-up". Those at the stage of "wannabes" want to be noticed and are the most likely to brag about their activities because that is exactly what the "wannabe" is—they want to be recognized as an active element in the community that is being noticed by the police and peers alike. Acknowledging an emerging "wannabe" presence may accelerate their efforts, but by their very public nature which is frequently accompanied by a name, it will also accelerate intelligence gathering and community-based efforts targeting both outreach and deterrence.

If you are a jurisdiction whose first contact with gangs is with those whom I have chosen to term "new-age", then your attempts at intervention will be most effective if you have maintained your community contacts because, at some level, the players involved will have some connection to your city by virtue of daily activities that occur where they live, work, or play-out their leisure time. The fluidity and mobility associated with new-age gangs makes them a particular challenge to police because their mobility forces police jurisdictions to be in closer contact in the sharing of information than ever before, while the dimension of fluidity among players delays the establishing of police investigative collaboration because of the "mix and match" configurations. Police investigations are being challenged to move from strategic planning to strategic thinking in response to new-age gang structure, but this is stifled by the difficulty in establishing a *modus operandi* that is reliant on regular and repeat participants who engage in criminal activity within a specific geographic area; neither of which is a characteristic of the new-age gang configuration.

About the Author

Cathy Prowse, Ph.D. is a former 25-year police officer with the Calgary Police Service, who currently holds an Adjunct Assistant Professor of Anthropology appointment at the University of Calgary. She is the recipient of local, national, and international recognition for her gang research which, over the course of her policing career and beyond, has been requested and used to inform expert testimony on four continents. As a result of her early work in this area, she was honored in 1996 by the International Association of Law Enforcement Intelligence Analysts for her writing of a police investigators' handbook titled, "Vietnamese Gangs: Fluidity and Mobility as Instruments of Organization"; the first individual Canadian to receive this honor. Due to its seminal nature, the distribution of her publication was limited to within the international law enforcement community to serve as an investigative tool into evolving gang structure; a gang structural prototype that is now being increasingly adopted by 21st century street gangs worldwide. Her expertise in the area of street gangs continues to be recognized; recently, she was part of an expert panel assembled by the Department of Justice Canada to provide advice on its youth-at-risk (of gangs/criminality) strategy. Dr. Prowse teaches in the Department of Anthropology at the University of Calgary and Mount Royal University; her research continues to focus on culturally influenced aspects of crime.

C. E. Prowse, *Defining Street Gangs in the 21st Century*, SpringerBriefs in Criminology,   53
DOI: 10.1007/978-1-4614-4307-0, © The Author(s) 2012

Glossary of Terminology

Action-set
- Linkages which exist in a street gang leader's total network and may be mobilized for a specific and limited purpose that is peripheral to, and in furtherance of, gang activity.
- *Text definition* An unorganized and generally youthful (under 18 years) collective of potential criminal participants, known to the street gang leader through a social network of relations. Street gang participation is peripheral and on an *ad hoc* basis; it does not form part of their self-identification.

Close-knit Network
- Defined as: 'A' knows or has contact with 'B'; 'B' knows or has contact with 'C'; and 'C' knows or has contact with 'A' independent of 'B' or any intermediate contact. Close-knit networks show redundancy in connectedness in that, there exists much overlap between contacts.

Coalition
- A temporary alliance of distinct parties for a limited purpose of a non-criminal type.

"Follow"
- An *emic* or insider's terminology used by street gang leaders to reference affiliation with an organized crime group. It can also be applied to street gang players who participate in criminal activity with a street gang leader for an indeterminate period of time.

Loose-knit Network
- Defined as: 'A' knows 'B'; 'B' knows 'C'; 'C' does not know 'A'. No redundancy is evident in the network, therefore mediating links are critical to understanding.

Network
- Includes all or some of the social unit—individuals and groups—with whom a particular individual or group is in contact.

C. E. Prowse, *Defining Street Gangs in the 21st Century*, SpringerBriefs in Criminology, 55
DOI: 10.1007/978-1-4614-4307-0, © The Author(s) 2012

New-Age Gang

- *Text definition* A loose-knit and fluid group of associates who comprise a subset of a street gang leader's enduring social network and who are preferentially activated in the commission of street-based criminal activity through that street gang leader. A gang identity does not form part of their collective self-identification.

Organized Crime Group

- *Text definition* A close-knit, geographically anchored group of enduring criminal associations, engaged in low-risk and high-gain criminal enterprise while also operating in the legal marketplace.

Partial Network

- Any extract of the total network based on some criterion applicable throughout the whole network.

Personal Network

- A set of ego-centred linkages which exist simultaneously on the basis of different interests and which persist beyond the duration of any particular transaction.

Quasi-group

- Action-sets which persist through a series of contexts of activity without any formal basis for membership can be considered 'quasi-groups'.

Sets

- Exist within ego-centred networks and are those individuals classified by ego according to a specific criterion.